A
Unde
Leaders

JACQUELINE V. TWILLIE

Ola Archway Publishing
2023

Acknowledgments

There is a wise quote that says, "No one achieves success alone."

I have experienced the truth in this quote repeatedly in my life. I'd like to express with deep gratitude all the mentors in my life who have shared wisdom with me, and that's helped me to realize that I should share this knowledge in written words with others.

My first school principal Mrs. Gwen Wade, and my transition from college to career mentor, Mr. and Mrs. Kelvin Henry. To the mentors who have been instrumental in helping me to step into a higher version of myself Suzy Batiz, Jack Manning Bancroft, Lakiesha Massey, and Lalah Delia deepest gratitude for your wisdom.

I'd also like to express gratitude to my editor Torres, you took this project head on and it has been a joy to work *with* you.

Table of Contents

Introduction ix

An Overview of the R4 Framework xv
Systematic Challenges xvi
Intersectional Challenges xviii
Mental Gymnastics xxii
Responsibilities of Corporations xxiv

The Resilient Leaders Manifesto xxix

Chapter 1: Embracing Change: The Power of Resilient Leadership ... 1
Change Can Be Your Ally 4
Underrepresented and Leadership Challenges 7
   Navigating Uncertainty: Taking Risks and Embracing New Ideas 12
   Leading Through Change: Inspiring Others to Embrace
   Transformation 14
      Resilient Leader Profile: Carla Harris 15
   Nurturing Change on a Personal Level 16

Chapter 2: Cultivating a Growth Mindset: Unlocking Your Potential 21
   The Power of a Growth Mindset: Embracing Setbacks
   and Failures 23
   Continuous Learning and Development: Enhancing Your
   Skills and Abilities 25
   From Limiting Beliefs to Limitless Potential:
   Overcoming Self-Doubt 28
      Resilient Leader Profile: Serena Williams 30

Chapter 3: Fostering Collaboration: Building Inclusive and Supportive Environments 33
   The 5 Strengths of Collaboration: Embracing Unique
   Talents and Perspectives 38

Unapologetic Leadership 40
Owning the Power of Being An Underrepresented Leader:
Creativity and Cultural Celebration... 46
Embracing Joy: The Path to Authenticity and Cultural
Celebration in Resilient Leadership 48
    Resilient Leader Profile: Shonda Rhimes - Masterful
    Storyteller and Trailblazing Producer.................................... 51
    Resilient Leader Profile: Bozoma Saint John......................... 57

Chapter 4: Empowering Others: First Unleashing the Potential Within 59
Empowerment in Leadership: Trusting Oneself to Make a
Difference... 61
Developing Leadership in Others: Opportunities for
Growth and Achievement.. 62
    Resilient Leader Profile: Valeisha Butterfield-Jones 64
Unapologetic Self-Advocacy: Empowering Yourself and
Others to Succeed... 66
    Resilient Leader Profile: Eric Thomas, The Hip Hop Preacher..... 67

Chapter 5: Cultivating Self-Awareness: The Key to Authentic Leadership 71
The Power of Self-Awareness: Understanding Your Impact on Others... 74
Reflective Leadership: Evaluating Behaviors and Actions 78
Leading with Purpose: Aligning Actions with Values 83
    Resilient Leader Strategy for Enhancing Value Awareness 85
    The Importance of Clarity in Values 89

Chapter 6: Boosting Resilience: Strengthening Your Inner Core... 95
Resilience in a Changing World: Adapting and Thriving 97
Self-Care and Well-being: Nurturing Your Resilience................. 100
    Burnout and the Fallout 102
Support Systems and Strategies: Building Resilient Teams 103
    Resilient Leader Profile: Thasunda Brown Duckett -
    Empowering Financial Leader and Catalyst for Change 103

Chapter 7: Inspiring Hope: Communicating with Impact 107
The Power of Hope: Motivating and Inspiring Others..................... 110

Leading with Growth Mindset: Creating Positive Work Boundaries ... 112
    Resilient Leader Profile: Nedra Glover Tawwab 114
Embracing Fear: Inspiring Hope for Success and Growth 115

Chapter 8: Risk, Resilience & Reward: Embracing Challenges for Growth 119
Calculated Risks: Balancing Ambition and Prudence 121
    Resilient Leader Profile: Rosalind Brewer 123
Resilience in the Face of Challenges: Overcoming Obstacles for Reward 125
    Rewards of Being Resilient 125
Celebrating Success: Acknowledging and Embracing the Rewards of Resilience 130

Chapter 9: Building Trust & Vision Setting: Creating a Foundation for Success 133
The Importance of Trust: Building and Cultivating Strong Team Relationships 135
Imagination to Vision: Aligning Action 136
Emulating Excellence: Adjusting Vision and Fostering Continuous Values Alignment 138
    Resilient Leader Profile: Thasunda Brown Duckett 140

Chapter 10: Business & Personal Negotiation: Advocating for Success 143
Introducing the L.A.T.T.E. Negotiation Framework 145
The Art of Negotiation: Strategies for Effective Business Negotiations 146
Self-Advocacy in Negotiations: Navigating Personal and Professional Goals 149
    Resilient Leader Profile: Shellye Archambeau 152
Win-Win Solutions: Conflict Navigations 153

Chapter 11: Team Building Conflict Management: Navigating Differences for Collaboration 159
    Resilient Leader Profile: Clarence Avant 162
Building Habits: Trust, Communication, Conflict, and Collaboration 164

Resilient Conflict Navigation Circle: Turning Differences
into Opportunities 166
What's Your Story: Harnessing the Strength of Different
Perspectives 168

Chapter 12: Strategic Networking & Partnerships: Creating Connections for Success 171
The Harmony of Strategic Networking: Building Relationships
Upon Resonance 174
Cultivating Unlikely Partnerships: Leveraging Collective Strengths..... 175
Strategic Networking & Partnerships 177
Collaboration for Impact: Creating Shared Value through
Strategic Alliances... 183
    Resilient Leader Profile: Jack Manning Bancroft 184

Chapter 13: Dear Resilient Leader: Embrace Your Journey.......... 187
Embracing Resilient Leadership: Resilient Organizational Culture...... 189
Taking Action: Applying Resilient Leadership Principles in
Your Journey 191
  The R4 Framework Checklist: Risk, Resilience, Reward,
  and Reset.. 194
    Risk Assessment: 194
    Resilience Building: 195
    Seeking Rewards: 195
    Reset:... 195
Shaping the Future: Inspiring, Empowering, and Uplifting Others..... 196

INTRODUCTION

Dear Resilient Leaders,

As leaders from underrepresented backgrounds, we know all too well the challenges of navigating predominantly white male workplaces. The struggle to be heard, recognized, and respected can be exhausting and discouraging. However, we can't let these challenges hold us back from achieving our goals and positively impacting our organizations.

I am excited to introduce the R4 framework. This strategy is designed to promote risk-taking and resilience, receiving our due rewards for our efforts, and rejuvenating our bodies and minds as we pursue our objectives. These are the basic elements to sustain our energy and maintain a fulfilling career while leaving our organizations in a stronger and healthier position than ever before.

Risk-taking: As resilient leaders, we must be willing to take risks and step outside our comfort zones. Embracing risk can lead to new opportunities and growth, and it can help us gain the visibility and recognition we deserve. Be bold, speak up, share your ideas, and take on new challenges.

Resilience: Navigating male-dominated workplaces can be challenging, and we must remain resilient to overcome obstacles and keep moving forward. Resilience is not about being immune to failure or setbacks; it's about bouncing back stronger and more determined than before. Remember that setbacks are not failures but opportunities to learn and grow.

Rewards: It's important to celebrate our successes and recognize our accomplishments, no matter how small they may seem. Celebrating our successes helps to build momentum and motivation to keep pushing forward. And it's also important to advocate for ourselves and negotiate for the compensation and recognition we deserve.

Reset: Finally, it's essential to prioritize rest and build healthy habits to reset and recharge. Self-care is vital to sustaining our energy and avoiding burnout. Take breaks, prioritize mental and physical health, and be surrounded by supportive networks.

As resilient leaders, we have the power to make a positive impact on our organizations and pave the way for future generations to dismantle the barriers we face so that future generations can focus on creativity and being. The aim of the R4 framework is one of many paths to building fulfilling careers that leave our organizations in a better position than ever.

Let's level the playing field.

Male-dominated industries refer to sectors or fields where white men hold most of the positions, especially those that significantly influence decision-making processes. The unfortunate reality is that almost every industry fits this description. Examples include—but are not limited to—technology, engineering, finance, construction, and politics. Historically, these sectors have been dominated by men, with women and other underrepresented groups facing significant barriers to entry and advancement.

Leaders from underrepresented groups are increasingly conscious of this gender disparity in male-dominated industries for several reasons. Firstly, recognizing the lack of diversity helps highlight the need for equal opportunities and representation. By acknowledging the gender imbalance, leaders can work towards creating inclusive environments where individuals from all backgrounds can thrive and contribute their unique perspectives.

My passion for equipping leaders from underrepresented groups to thrive regardless of industry stems from my experiences and challenges as a Black American woman. I recognize that members of racialized and gendered groups have historically been left outside positions of power. This means they often encounter biases, stereotypes, limited access to resources and mentorship in professional settings. While this book is written for those who identify with gender and racial terms, I recognize that I do not have the expertise yet to address some of the unique challenges faced by gender non-conforming people; nonetheless, I believe that those of you who are members of this latter group will be able to identify with many of the issues and solutions discussed in this book

By providing support and training, leaders can empower underrepresented groups to overcome these obstacles and succeed in male-dominated industries.

Moreover, being conscious of the racial and gender disparities in these industries allows leaders to challenge and dismantle systemic barriers. It involves promoting policies that encourage diversity, implementing inclusive hiring practices, and advocating for equal pay and opportunities for career advancement. I know leaders can create environments that value and benefit from the contributions of individuals from diverse backgrounds. To make this happen, it will require leaders who are dedicated to fostering a culture that accepts differences, even when it requires personal or organizational change.

Ultimately, being aware of racialized and gendered disparities in male-dominated industries should lead to taking action to address them. It's beyond time that we take meaningful action to achieve gender equality and create a more inclusive society. Leaders like myself and thousands of others play a crucial role in driving this change by listening to underrepresented groups and providing the necessary tools, knowledge, and support to excel in these industries. Doing so paves the way for a more diverse and equitable workforce, where everyone has an equal chance to succeed, regardless of gender or background.

As I look back over my career as a leader in a male-dominated industry, navigating new initiatives and changes in the workplace was especially challenging. I was disappointed in how easy it was to feel overwhelmed or discouraged, particularly when faced with uncertainty and the need to take calculated risks. I began my career during the Great Recession when ish was hitting the economic fan. However, by adopting a framework that focuses on risk, resilience, reward, and reset, I slowly found a path that, in hindsight, I noticed would enable me to sustain my energy and build a fulfilling career while leaving organizations in a more robust and healthier position than before.

Through the guidance of my personal board of directors, I learned that healthy career risks are essential to growth and advancement; managing the risks and ensuring they align with my values and career goals was the cornerstone. Building resilience and seeking resources to ease the change transition became equally important. Subconsciously, I began to develop a resilient mindset, which helped me quickly adapt to new systems, overcome obstacles, and focus on achieving the initial goals of the teams I was a part of.

After coaching underrepresented leaders around the globe, I've seen that the primary goal of most initiatives is to achieve a reward, whether it's increased revenue, making a positive impact in the world, customer satisfaction, employee engagement, or a combination of all of the above. Setting clear goals and measuring progress is vital to ensure the initiative succeeds. Yet, it's equally important to have a personal plan to reset so you can celebrate successes, evaluate what worked and what didn't, and recharge for the next challenge. Without a focus on the leader's mindset and relationship to resilience, it can be a lonely road.

As you read this book, I advise you to take what you need and drop anything that doesn't align. There's no one-size-fits-all approach to leadership, and I intend for this book to be a collection of tips that will aid in formulating your leadership strategy on resilience.

Sincerely,

Jacqueline V. Twillie
Founder of ZeroGap.co
Creator of the Resilient Leaders Program

AN OVERVIEW OF THE R4 FRAMEWORK

A leader's response to challenges will shift as life experiences influence decision-making. Resilience will be strengthened or weakened based on tools available during times of challenge. Activating resilience muscles is similar to using a compass; it is one of many helpful tools in decision-making. The R4 framework focuses on taking calculated risks, building resilience, achieving rewards, and resetting one's intentions. This is a circular tool to help with decision-making or navigating change at any scale. The R4 framework is designed to help underrepresented leaders navigate male-dominated industries with self-efficacy, driving the process to build a fulfilling career and impact organizations in a more robust and healthier position.

Before diving into the substance of this book, I'd like to share the baseline definitions I'm using for the R4 system. You can refer to these definitions whenever these concepts appear in the following chapters.

Risk refers to exposure to danger or possible harm, loss, or adverse outcomes. It can also mean exposing someone or something valuable to such hazards. Resilience has two primary definitions. First, it refers to the capacity of an individual or an institution to withstand or recover quickly from difficulties, demonstrating toughness and adaptability. Second, it can refer to the ability of a substance or object to spring back into shape, indicating elasticity. A reward is a recognition for one's service, effort, or achievement. It can take various forms: prizes, money, awards, honors, gifts, or any other valuable or beneficial item or experience. Reset is a verb that means to set something again or differently. It can be applied to various contexts, such as resetting an alarm to a new time. In electronics, it can also refer to causing a binary device to enter the state representing the numeral zero.

The R4 framework provides a systematic approach for leaders to navigate decision-making processes when facing challenges or changes. It encourages careful consideration of risks, the development of resilience, the pursuit of rewards, and the prioritization of rest and reflection. By utilizing this framework, leaders can effectively process challenges, accept rewards, and reset their energy, leading to more successful outcomes and personal growth despite challenges.

SYSTEMATIC CHALLENGES

Many leadership books fail to go beyond the acknowledgment that underrepresented leaders are not at fault for the systemic challenges they face in workplaces. These challenges stem from historical and societal factors that have created unequal access to opportunities and resources. It's not often discussed how the lingering impact of colonization is a driver of current dynamics that industries are white male-dominated. When the discussion of systematic challenges comes up at a conference or within an association about diversity statistics, there is a discussion surrounding historical discrimination and bias in recruitment and hiring practices and calls for commitment to change. It is well documented that many industries were closed to people of color and women, which led to a lack of diversity in the workforce, and decades later, we still see announcements of the first gender or race to reach. While we celebrate the leaders from under-represented groups, who achieve these "first of" accomplishments, the road to stay in those positions is paved with an advanced set of systematic challenges.

It's more than a cliche to say we must be "comfortable being uncomfortable." Social and cultural norms that have played a role in perpetuating leadership teams that are white-male dominated are still the majority of what's reflected in many industries. Stereotypes and biases create barriers to entry for people who have been left outside the margins of power and discourage them from pursuing careers in certain industries. For example, there may be a belief that women are not suited to particular roles or that people of color lack the necessary qualifications. This bias, whether conscious or unconscious, perpetuates a selection of candidates that are a " fit culturally," which tends to fit with male dominance.

The lack of diversity in leadership requires a multi-faceted approach. It involves recognizing and addressing historical discrimination and biases, creating inclusive and equitable recruitment and hiring practices, promoting representation, mentorship in leadership positions, and mental well-being support that expands outside the office setting. This is not the burden or responsibility of the leader in the underrepresented group to set up but instead the responsibility of the men who currently sit in positions that must become brave enough to use their powers to drive the change.

Let's explore examples of systematic challenges faced by underrepresented leaders. Bias in hiring and promotions can hinder the selection of qualified individuals for positions, whether these biases are unconscious or conscious. This issue is well documented in research papers from McKinsey to Stanford, yet the road to equity remains saddled with the debris of generational exclusion. Another issue is the persistent wage gap between different demographic groups, with underrepresented leaders often receiving lower pay than their counterparts. At the same time, there is progress in pay transparency methods; the gap is stubborn and persistent. Without a transparent pay policy, underrepresented will continue to negotiate for themselves with a partial data set. Stereotyping also poses a challenge, as underrepresented leaders may encounter biases based on perceived capabilities or differences from the dominant group, leading to discrimination. In most cases, the discrimination is subtle, but it remains a primary challenge to address. Additionally, inadequate policies and practices in the workplace contribute to the difficulty faced by underrepresented leaders, highlighting the need for more inclusive measures that address their unique challenges and enhance their chances of success.

It is essential to recognize these systematic challenges and work towards creating more equitable and inclusive workplaces. This requires a collective effort from all organization members to challenge biases, promote diversity, and support underrepresented leaders in their career development. Equally important is maintaining the burden of solving these challenges onto the back of the underrepresented leaders. Their voice should influence the design of equitable systems, and white male leaders in organizations must take action.

INTERSECTIONAL CHALLENGES

Beyond the systematic challenges that underrepresented leaders face, various intersectional challenges must be explored and solutions diverged from. These challenges arise from the overlapping identities and forms of marginalization experienced by individuals with multiple minority statuses. The term "intersectional" was coined by Kimberlé Crenshaw, a legal scholar, in the late 1980s. Intersectionality refers to the concept that individuals' experiences of social inequality and oppression cannot be understood or addressed adequately by considering only a single axis of identity, such as race or gender. Instead, it emphasizes the interconnectedness and interplay of multiple social categories, such as race, gender, class, sexuality, etc.

Intersectionality recognizes that individuals may experience overlapping forms of discrimination and disadvantage based on the intersections of their identities. For example, a black woman may face unique challenges distinct from those faced by white women or black men, as the intersection of race and gender shapes her experiences. Acknowledging these intersecting identities and their complexities, intersectionality highlights the need for a more nuanced and comprehensive understanding of social inequalities and the systems perpetuating them.

On the axis of intersectional areas that Resilient Leaders face, stereotype threats pose a significant challenge for underrepresented leaders as they grapple with the fear of reinforcing negative stereotypes tied to their identity. This fear adds pressure and anxiety and could result in decreased confidence and performance. The impact of stereotype threat can impede effective leadership and contribute to burnout.

Underrepresented leaders often find themselves caught in a double bind, navigating conflicting expectations based on their intersecting identities. For instance, Black women may be deemed too assertive if they exhibit leadership qualities typically associated with white men or not assertive enough if they lead with empathy or compassion. These conflicting expectations can make it difficult for underrepresented leaders to strike a balance and be perceived positively. This double bind makes it nearly impossible to make a mistake, which is an unrealistic expectation of perfection.

Furthermore, underrepresented leaders often require support to represent their identity in a leadership position. The lack of representation can lead to feelings of isolation and increased pressure to advocate for and represent their marginalized group. This emotional burden can be taxing and limit their access to supportive networks. Bias and discrimination are more likely to affect underrepresented leaders due to their intersecting identities. They may encounter challenges such as subtle biases, exclusion, and being overlooked for opportunities. These experiences undermine their authority, erode trust, and hinder team cohesion, resulting in heightened stress and strain. Achieving work-life integration poses unique challenges for underrepresented leaders, given societal expectations and cultural norms associated with their identities. Balancing work responsibilities, family obligations, and personal well-being can be particularly demanding, leading to increased stress and burnout.

It is essential to recognize that the intersectional challenges faced by underrepresented leaders can vary depending on race, gender, ethnicity, sexual orientation, and other aspects of identity. These challenges underscore the importance of fostering inclusive environments that support and empower underrepresented leaders to thrive and succeed.

The importance of representation cannot be understated. Despite ongoing efforts to promote inclusivity, underrepresented leaders face numerous challenges that hinder their progress and success. In 2020, during the early stages of the Global pandemic and in the aftermath of George Floyd's murder, organizations rushed to signal their support of racial and social justice initiatives. They shared black squares as a gesture of solidarity on social media; they issued rhetoric supporting Black Lives and made bold pledges to implement equity practices for underrepresented leaders and entrepreneurs. Three years later, most organizations fell far short of their ambitious promises.

The changes marginalized communities needed—and so many corporations claimed to support—required consistent action, not just rhetoric. Instead of steadfast support, however, entire Diversity, Equity, and Inclusion teams were laid off as cost-saving measures amidst economic uncertainty. The data goes deeper into the challenges, amplifying five key obstacles that underrepresented leaders face: lack of representation, bias, discrimination, limited network access, imposter syndrome, and microaggressions. This book aims to shed light on the harsh realities that underrepresented leaders encounter and emphasizes the need for collective action to address these issues.

Underrepresented leaders often find themselves in environments where their identities are in the minority. This lack of representation can make finding internal organizational support systems that understand their unique experiences and offer solutions to such challenges. The absence of diverse perspectives in decision-making processes can also perpetuate systemic biases and limit opportunities for advancement for leaders of underrepresented groups.

Bias and discrimination persist in many organizations, creating substantial barriers for underrepresented leaders. Stereotypes and prejudices can lead to unfair evaluations, unequal access to opportunities, and limited career progression. The burden of disproving these biases falls on the underrepresented individual, requiring them to consistently prove their worth and abilities in the face of biased perceptions. The double bind presents itself again with an unattainable expectation of perfection.

Imposter syndrome, characterized by feelings of self-doubt and inadequacy despite evident accomplishments, affects underrepresented leaders disproportionately. I liken this to professional gas "not enough," resulting in the underrepresented leader questioning their value to the organization's goals. The constant need to prove oneself in an environment where their presence may be questioned can lead to internalized doubts and anxiety. The fear of not being perfect can translate into behavior identified as imposter syndrome, which in turn can hinder confidence, decision-making, and overall performance.

Coupled with experiences of microaggressions, which are subtle, often unintentional acts or comments that marginalize and invalidate underrepresented individuals. These subtle forms of discrimination can erode self-esteem, create a hostile work environment, and hinder professional growth. The cumulative effect of repeated microaggressions can lead to increased stress, reduced job satisfaction, and a sense of isolation.

The challenges faced by underrepresented leaders are authentic and multifaceted. Addressing these issues requires a collective effort from organizations, leaders, and society. Companies must actively work towards creating inclusive cultures, eliminating biases, and fostering diversity at all levels. Promoting representation, offering mentorship programs, and challenging microaggressions are crucial steps toward leveling the playing field. Recognizing and valuing the contributions of underrepresented leaders benefits not only individuals but also organizations, as diverse perspectives lead to innovation, improved decision-making, and enhanced business outcomes. Acknowledging and addressing these challenges can create a more equitable and inclusive future for all.

MENTAL GYMNASTICS

The journey of an underrepresented leader in a white male-dominated industry is fraught with challenges that extend far beyond professional expertise. Navigating microaggressions requires a unique set of mental gymnastics—cognitive strategies and emotional resilience that underrepresented leaders employ to maintain their self-worth, address biases, and persevere in pursuit of success. Later in the book, we delve into the tools underrepresented leaders use to navigate microaggressions and shed light on their incredible resilience in adversity.

Underrepresented leaders often develop a heightened sense of self-awareness, allowing them to recognize when microaggressions occur and understand the underlying motivations or biases behind them. Additionally, cultivating emotional intelligence empowers leaders to manage their emotional responses, maintaining composure in challenging situations. This self-awareness and emotional intelligence are fundamental in navigating microaggressions without compromising personal well-being.

Resilient leaders are skilled at selecting their battles wisely when confronted with microaggressions. They understand that addressing every instance may be mentally and emotionally draining. Instead, they strategically choose which battles to fight, focusing on those that have the potential to create meaningful change. By responding constructively, they aim to educate and raise awareness, challenging biases while preserving their mental energy.

Creating a robust support network is crucial for underrepresented leaders facing microaggressions. Surrounding themselves with mentors and allies who understand their unique experiences and challenges provides a safe space for validation, advice, and emotional support. These networks serve as an invaluable source of strength and encouragement, bolstering resilience in the face of ongoing microaggressions.

Resilient leaders actively engage in self-affirmation and celebrate their accomplishments to counteract the negative impact of microaggressions. Acknowledging their strengths, skills, and contributions reinforces their self-worth and builds resilience. Engaging in positive self-talk, practicing self-care, and seeking validation from within help underrepresented leaders maintain a strong sense of self amidst the microaggressions they encounter.

Resilient leaders often embrace the role of advocates and change agents within their organizations and industries. They leverage their experiences with microaggressions to bring about systemic change, advocating for diversity, inclusion, and equity. By actively participating in diversity initiatives and mentorship programs and raising awareness of microaggressions, they strive to create more supportive and inclusive environments for future generations.

Navigating microaggressions as an underrepresented leader in a white male-dominated industry requires mental gymnastics—strategic thinking, emotional resilience, and self-empowerment. By employing tools such as self-awareness, selective battles, support networks, self-affirmation, and advocacy, underrepresented leaders persevere and strive to overcome the barriers and biases they encounter. Organizations and industries must recognize and address the microaggressions faced by underrepresented leaders, fostering inclusive cultures that value diversity and provide equal opportunities for all. We can dismantle the barriers that hinder progress and create an environment where underrepresented leaders can thrive through collective effort and ongoing dialogue.

RESPONSIBILITIES OF CORPORATIONS

The role of CEOs and boards of directors in supporting underrepresented leaders is crucial in fostering belonging alongside diversity, inclusion, and equity within organizations. Absent of accountability of white male leaders who currently hold leadership positions and power, underrepresented leaders face a hamster wheel of performative corporate press releases and annual reports with no change to business systems.

CEOs and board members play a vital role in setting the tone for fostering diversity and inclusion as core values within the organization. Their commitment to championing these values is crucial in creating an environment that promotes and supports underrepresented leaders. It requires honest dialogue about one's beliefs and relationship to power. Executives should embrace their responsibilities in setting the tone for rapidly accelerating belonging and equity in leadership positions.

CEOs and board members should clearly articulate the vision and commitment to diversity and inclusion. They should communicate that creating a diverse and inclusive workforce is a moral imperative and a strategic business advantage. By aligning the organization's mission and values with diversity and inclusion, they send a powerful message to employees at all levels. They should actively engage in inclusive behaviors, promote equal opportunities, and demonstrate respect for diverse perspectives. By modeling inclusive leadership, they inspire others within the organization to do the same and create a culture of inclusion. A popular strategy is linking annual bonuses to the metrics of DEIB as a powerful way to move beyond performative metrics.

Additionally, executives in the C-Suite communicate and demonstrate with actions the business case for belonging, diversity, and inclusion. In annual reports, there should be a noticeable articulation of the benefits of having a diverse workforce, including enhanced innovation, improved decision-making, and increased customer satisfaction. They can garner stakeholder support by highlighting diversity's positive impact on organizational performance.

Sustained allocation of resources to support diversity and inclusion initiatives. This includes investing in diversity training programs, employee resource groups, mentorship and sponsorship programs, and other DEIB initiatives promoting underrepresented leaders' development and advancement. By allocating resources, CEOs demonstrate their commitment and provide the necessary support for driving change even during economic uncertainty. This can look like setting ten to twenty-year road maps instead of 18 to 36-month metrics.

Board members must hold leadership accountable for diversity and inclusion outcomes. They should establish metrics and goals to track progress and regularly assess the organization's diversity and inclusion efforts. Holding leaders responsible for creating inclusive teams and promoting underrepresented leaders ensures that diversity and inclusion remain prioritized throughout all economic states. Moreover, it promotes transparency by reporting on the organization's diversity and inclusion efforts. This includes sharing demographic data, progress reports, and best practices. Transparent reporting without data manipulation holds the organization accountable and allows stakeholders to assess the organization's commitment to diversity and inclusion.

CEOs and board members are responsible for setting the tone from the top by championing diversity and inclusion as core values. By demonstrating their commitment, leading by example, communicating the business case, allocating resources, holding leaders accountable, and promoting transparency, they create an inclusive culture that values and encourages underrepresented leaders. Their active involvement fosters an environment where diversity and inclusion thrive, and underrepresented leaders can lead with the saddled burdens of racial, gender, or sexual orientation bias.

No shortage of research provides blueprints for a transformational business culture that removes barriers for underrepresented leaders. These concepts include but are not limited to incorporating inclusive policies and practices: CEOs and board members can drive change by establishing policies and procedures supporting underrepresented leaders. This includes implementing inclusive hiring and promotion practices, ensuring pay equity, and providing diverse leadership development programs. Creating a level playing field enables underrepresented leaders to thrive and advance within the organization.

CEOs and board members can participate in mentorship and sponsorship programs for underrepresented leaders. By providing guidance, support, and advocacy, they help cultivate talent and create opportunities for advancement. Mentoring relationships and sponsorship connections can significantly impact an individual's career trajectory and increase organizational visibility.

CEOs and board members should actively work to address organizational biases. As a core function of their role, they oversee the implementation of diversity training programs, raise awareness about unconscious biases, and create accountability mechanisms to ensure fair and unbiased decision-making. They create an environment that supports underrepresented leaders by promoting a culture of inclusivity and challenging preconceptions.

CEOs and board members can collaborate with external organizations and partners to support underrepresented leaders. This includes participating in industry-wide initiatives, supporting diversity-focused organizations, and leveraging networks to create opportunities for underrepresented talent beyond their organizations. By working collectively, they can drive systemic change and promote inclusivity across industries.

Executives and board members can not delegate the support of underrepresented leaders to someone else within the organization. They have the power and influence to drive change, foster inclusivity, and create opportunities for underrepresented individuals to thrive. By championing diversity and inclusion, allocating resources, providing mentorship and sponsorship, and promoting equal opportunities, executives and board members can empower underrepresented leaders to succeed and contribute their unique perspectives. This summary highlights the importance of the C-Suite role and sets the stage for a section of the book that celebrates the achievements and stories of underrepresented leaders.

THE RESILIENT LEADERS MANIFESTO

We, resilient leaders, believe in creating an equitable and equal world where individuals who have traditionally been underrepresented in leadership can thrive, no matter the historical or systemic challenges.

We stand for

Embracing change: *We embrace change as an opportunity to grow, adapt, and evolve. We are not fearless yet; instead, we welcome fear and determine the wisest path in taking risks and embracing new ideas, even when uncertain or unpopular.*

Cultivating a growth mindset: *We believe that setbacks and failures are not permanent and that everyone can grow into the highest version of themselves by learning from setbacks. We embrace a growth mindset, enabling us to enhance our skills and abilities continuously.*

Fostering collaboration: *We believe collaboration is one of the keys to making the world more equitable. We celebrate each other's unique talents and perspectives. We work collaboratively with others to create supportive and inclusive work environments where everyone is seen and heard without apology for who they are. We applaud unapologetic leadership characteristics.*

Empowering others: *We believe in empowering others to make decisions that positively impact their own lives and the lives of their communities. We seek opportunities for individuals to develop their skills, take on new challenges, and achieve their full potential unapologetically.*

Cultivating self-awareness: *We believe in the power of self-awareness to inform our attitudes, habits, actions, and decisions. We reflect on our behaviors and work to understand our impact on others.*

Building resilience: *We believe resilience in a changing world is essential to impact society positively. We take proactive steps to strengthen our resilience, such as engaging in regular self-care practices, seeking support from others, and maintaining awareness of our goals and values.*

Inspiring hope: *We believe that hope is a powerful motivator and that we must encourage hope in each other. We communicate with fairness, positivity, and confidence and work to create a future full of promise and potential.*

By embracing these values, we can create a world where individuals and organizations can thrive, no matter their challenges. We are committed to being resilient leaders who inspire, empower, and uplift those around us.

Chapter 1

EMBRACING CHANGE: THE POWER OF RESILIENT LEADERSHIP

Dear Resilient Leader,

I hope this email finds you in good health and high spirits. As a leader from an underrepresented group, I understand the unique challenges you may face in navigating systemic obstacles while demonstrating resilience. In this book, I emphasize the importance of embracing change to unlock your power of resilient leadership in the face of these challenges.

In our ever-evolving workplaces, change is constant. Organizations grapple with disruptive technologies, global crises, and shifting market dynamics. As leaders, particularly those from underrepresented groups, we must recognize that our ability to embrace change directly influences our success and the success of those we lead.

Embracing change begins with acknowledging that it can be both exhilarating and uncomfortable. For leaders like us, change often challenges the established routines and the barriers and biases we encounter due to historical structures of power. However, during these times of change, we can tap into our power and exhibit resilient leadership.

Resilient leadership is not about naively accepting change or merely weathering the storm. It is about actively seeking growth and learning from the experience. By embracing change, we can uncover hidden strengths, enhance problem-solving skills, and inspire our teams to navigate uncertainty with confidence.

A prerequisite to the Resilient Leaders Program is reading Mindset: The Psychology of Success *by Dr. Carol Dweck. In this book, Dweck introduces the growth mindset concept, explains how to foster it in our daily lives, and how to begin viewing change as an opportunity rather than a threat. This book,* Dear Resilient Leaders, *incorporates many insights from Dweck's research and applies them to the experiences of underrepresented people in the workplace.*

If our teams are to embrace personal and organizational change, refining our communication as leaders is vital. Inside this book, we unpack the values associated with transparent communication. We will also discuss how to articulate the reasoning behind and the impact that will follow the changes we hope to implement. This includes encouraging open dialogue, listening actively, and addressing concerns or resistance with empathy. We emphasize the Resilient Leader's ability to recognize one's unique experiences can contribute valuable insights to guide your team through the challenges they may face.

This includes leading by example as a catalyst to inspire action. Resilient Leaders demonstrate adaptability by embracing change and showing a willingness to learn and evolve. The actions inspire and motivate team members to do the same. You, as Resilient Leaders, provide a leadership-in-action template for others facing similar obstacles.

Resilient Leadership never happens in a silo. Resilient leaders require resilient networks. As you go further into the book we delve into the importance of intentionally surrounding yourself with fellow leaders who have faced similar challenges. Leaders need each other to grow through collaboration and mentorship; through the sharing of experiences; through the exchange of ideas; and through and learning from one another's stories of perseverance. As we navigate systemic barriers, building alliances with other people from marginalized communities is one of the most powerful strategies at our disposal. History has demonstrated this time and time again.

To become a leader who stands out and makes a substantial difference through volatile market conditions, you must commit to continuous development. This means investing in yourself by cultivating the knowledge, skills, tools, and relationships you need to maneuver your professional world effectively. Seek professional development opportunities, attend workshops, and engage in ongoing learning to stay ahead of the curve. By constantly evolving your own capabilities, you will be better prepared to lead and advocate for change within your organization.

Remember, embracing change is a journey that requires courage, self-reflection, and a willingness to step outside your comfort zone. As a leader from an underrepresented group, you possess a unique perspective and the strength to navigate systemic challenges. By unlocking your personal power of resilient leadership, you will propel yourself forward and inspire those around you to do the same.

Let's create a future where change is seen as an opportunity to thrive and achieve remarkable success, regardless of the barriers we face. I wish you continued success and resilience on your leadership journey.

Jacqueline V. Twillie,
Founder of ZeroGap.co
Creator of the Resilient Leaders Program

CHANGE CAN BE YOUR ALLY

Change is an inevitable part of life. Depending on the circumstances, it can incite excitement and inspiration; it can just as easily be daunting, disruptive, and uncomfortable. When we discuss change in the workplace, it's often met with disdain. This attitude frequently stops from the highest levels of an organization. Leaders should maintain a high-level viewpoint which includes how systems are developed and the feedback loop that members of the organization engage with. This insight can open doors to communication and acknowledge feelings of change so that employees with less influence who are fearful to "rock the boat," even when the need for change is dire are able to adapt to change.

Within the Resilient Leaders program, we embrace taking risks. We understand that sometimes the wisest decisions are the ones that will uncover what we are afraid of and reveal new obstacles. We believe, furthermore, that challenges can be turned into opportunities for growth. This very idea is embedded in our manifesto. By adopting a growth mindset, leaders navigate uncertain times and become more in tune with the values that drive sound decision-making.

Admittedly, this kind of leadership is not always easy. That's why I can't overstate how crucial resilience is for navigating life's challenges. Resilience enables leaders to bounce back from setbacks with determination, learn from their experiences, and continue moving forward. It empowers them to adapt to change, embrace new opportunities, and lead their teams through uncertain times. Moreover, resilience helps leaders maintain supportive environments in which team members are inspired, innovation is encouraged, and the growth mindset thrives—even in the face of adversity.

The term "resilience" traces its origins back to the Latin word *"resilire,"* which means "to jump back" or "to rebound." This word aptly captures the idea of returning to an original position after being pressured or stressed. My experience in coaching underrepresented leaders has led me to believe that leaders who embrace their capacity for resilience are stronger and wiser due to the experience of being stretched. While the challenge is not required for the leader to grow, there are often ways to reframe the circumstances by boosting awareness of moving forward in the face of adversity.

A fundamental principle of embracing change is recognizing that it can catalyze personal development. When we resist change, we limit our potential, hindering our ability to adapt to new circumstances. On the other hand, by accepting change and viewing it as an opportunity, we open ourselves up to a world of possibilities.

Written into the job descriptions of leadership roles is the requirement of problem-solving. Challenges are a part of the daily task of leaders, presenting new obstacles and hurdles that require tapping into problem-solving skills. These challenges can range from shifts in technology and market trends to organizational restructuring or personal life transitions. Instead of being intimidated by these challenges, Resilient Leaders reframe them as learning opportunities. This is also known as the growth mindset, a philosophy we'll explore more in this book.

Rather than viewing setbacks as failures, a growth mindset can help us reimagine them as valuable learning experiences that help refine skills and approaches, allowing us to tap into curiosity. By understanding that challenges are not roadblocks but stepping stones, leaders can cultivate resilience and strengthen the necessary skills to thrive in a constantly changing environment.

Many of the Resilient Leaders Program graduates embrace the concept that opportunities often arise from moments of disruption and change. As the saying goes, "Necessity is the mother of invention." When faced with new challenges, thinking outside of the current viewpoint, exploring alternative solutions, and pushing boundaries of comfort. This mindset shift can lead to breakthrough innovations and novel approaches that would have otherwise remained untapped.

If there is one message I hope to convey to you, it is this: Embrace change effectively. Our core values as individuals and our leadership skills will be tested in periods of unrest and uncertainty. When these times come, it is vital that we keep our leadership practices and our convictions in alignment. Leveraging creative thinking skills allows for exploring new ideas and perspectives. Leaders uncover fresh insights and gain a deeper understanding of the changing landscape by seeking advice from diverse connections and being receptive to feedback. It supports a smooth transition in navigating through change when coupled with the ability to stay adaptable. For Resilient Leaders, this involves embracing ambiguity and working with the unknowns of change. Thus, the leader can embrace uncertainty by letting go of rigid expectations. Resilient leaders can seize new opportunities and adapt to evolving circumstances more effectively with an increased awareness of when to tap into the various skills in their toolbox.

In my book, *Don't Leave Money On The Table: Negotiation Strategies for Women Leaders*, I discuss the importance of forestalling challenges in a negotiation. When you can anticipate potential obstacles in the way of your objectives, you put yourself in the best possible position to envision the full range of outcomes and work towards the best one. Rather than waiting for change to happen, leaders take the initiative to prepare possible solutions. This involves staying informed about industry trends, reviewing available data, developing new skills, and actively seeking growth opportunities. When leaders use their imagination to transform obstacles into stepping stones, they gain the power to define—on their own terms—the metrics and meaning of success.

With that said, success cannot be achieved through monologue; a resilient leader understands the importance of dialogue and shared narratives of success. We must resist the temptation to move through the professional world as if we were on a solo hero's journey. Doing that requires building a support network to help us navigate change. This means surrounding ourselves with individuals who can guide us, encourage us, share our values, and understand our vision. Success isn't usually born from one mind alone; it requires the meeting of many minds too. We need the insight of others to open new doors of opportunity and avoid the mindset of, "We've always done it this way," which can cause us to overlook those doors. Therefore, collaborating with others rounds out the circle of essential resilient leadership habits.

Undoubtedly, change can be intimidating even after we've mastered these strategies. No amount of preparation or training can change that. However, if we avoid change, we often get caught in a reactionary mode of putting out fires once they've already started to burn. It is far better to face change squarely, learn how and when it appears in our lives, and embrace it as a critical ally in an ever-evolving world.

UNDERREPRESENTED AND LEADERSHIP CHALLENGES

As we explore how change is inevitable in any workplace, the corresponding leadership challenges can be even more pronounced for individuals from traditionally underrepresented demographics; such leaders often find themselves grappling with additional pressure to prove their worth and overcome prevailing stereotypes and biases. In the face of organizational transformations, resilient leaders may experience heightened stress and anxiety as the fear of failure looms. For instance, Karla, a black female executive taking on a senior leadership role in a male-dominated tech company, might feel the weight of expectations and constantly strive to prove her technical expertise and decision-making abilities.

In male-dominated industries, resilient leaders from underrepresented demographics often encounter intersectional obstacles when navigating change in the workplace. They may face heightened scrutiny and the need to demonstrate their competence and capabilities to constantly counter prevailing biases. For instance, a British person leading a construction company through a period of organizational restructuring might encounter skepticism from their colleagues, who may question her ability to make tough decisions or manage large-scale projects. Such external pressure, combined with the internal desire to succeed and challenge societal norms, can intensify the stress and anxiety experienced by resilient leaders in the face of change.

The fear of failure can be a significant source of stress for resilient leaders in male-dominated industries, exacerbating the challenges associated with workplace leadership. These leaders are often acutely aware of the higher stakes in their roles as they strive to break down barriers and pave the way for future generations. When the leader is a lone representative of their gender or race, the weight of their actions can impact future hiring decisions. The leader feels an unspoken burden to represent all people who identify with similar demographics. While unfair and unrealistic to represent all people, it's an everyday reality for lone leaders. For example, a Black executive who has worked tirelessly to establish credibility and gain acceptance within a predominantly white male finance firm may grapple with immense fear of making a mistake that could impact future hiring decisions of Black candidates. They may worry that any misstep or setback could reinforce negative stereotypes or diminish the progress made by others in their demographic. This threat of failure can become a constant agitator, heightening the stress and pressure resilient leaders face as they navigate change in their professional lives.

The pressure to prove themselves, overcome biases and stereotypes, and the fear of failure can significantly impact their experiences during organizational change. By acknowledging and addressing these challenges, organizations can create a more inclusive and supportive environment that enables all leaders to thrive, regardless of race, gender, or background. Throughout this book, I'll float between the language of everyday leadership and resilient leadership strategies. This two-pronged approach intends to provide resilient leaders with tools to pull from throughout their leadership journey.

An everyday leadership challenge is rolling out a company-wide process that changes how individuals contribute to work. Such change can lead a team to fear losing control, increasing uncertainty about job responsibilities and extending expectations. This uncertainty can lead to fear, and anxiety may not be as efficient as expected in adapting to new systems. A tool that resilient leaders can use to navigate this challenge is to work towards establishing new feedback loops that can help boost resilience, allowing individuals to adjust more effectively to change. Feedback loops allow for constant evaluation and adjustment, which can help individuals feel more in control and empowered during periods of change. In addition to establishing new feedback loops, promoting resilience requires adopting a growth mindset, developing grit, and regulating neurotransmitters.

Grit refers to the ability to persevere in facing challenges and adversity. It involves passion and perseverance, even when the going gets tough. Developing determination supports resilient leaders to remain committed to their goals, even during difficult times. In Psychologist Angela Duckworth's TED Talk, she describes grit web of skills: "Grit is passion and perseverance for very long-term goals. Grit is having stamina. Grit is sticking with your future, day in, day out, not just for the week, not just for the month, but for years, and working really hard to make that future a reality. Grit is living life like it's a marathon, not a sprint." Resilient leaders who increase their awareness of stressors during change can tap into grit as they navigate the complexity of underrepresented workplace dynamics.

Resilient leaders navigating interpersonal challenges while rolling out change processes must also know their team members' motivators to help them overcome hurdles to accept change. For example, some employees resist buying into a new approach because that change disrupts the routines and habits people have developed. This is because established habits provide comfort and familiarity, and changing them can be disorienting. Additionally, the uncertainty that comes with a process change can be unsettling. People may need to learn what to expect, how long the transition will last, or how it will impact their job or responsibilities. Finally, changing processes can lead to a sense of loss of control. People may feel they have no say in the matter, and this lack of power can be distressing. Keeping this in mind, leaders can lay the groundwork for establishing new feedback loops.

Establishing new feedback loops for habits can help individuals adapt to change more effectively. Feedback loops provide information on how well a person does and can help guide behavior. In the context of changing processes at work, establishing new feedback loops can help individuals stay on track and feel more in control. For example, if a person is learning a new software program, setting small goals and receiving feedback on progress can help them feel more in control and motivated. Additionally, establishing new feedback loops can help individuals identify areas where they need to improve and adjust.

The Role of Neurotransmitters

Neurotransmitters play an essential role in promoting resilience. Neurotransmitters are chemicals in the brain that help transmit signals between neurons. Serotonin, dopamine, and norepinephrine are three neurotransmitters that are particularly important for promoting resilience. Serotonin helps regulate mood and is associated with feelings of happiness and well-being. Dopamine is associated with motivation and reward-seeking behavior.

Norepinephrine is associated with the body's stress response and can help individuals stay aware and focused in the face of challenges. Serotonin, dopamine, and norepinephrine neurotransmitters promote resilience by regulating mood, motivation, and stress response. By understanding these factors, leaders can help themselves and their teams navigate change more effectively.

There are several common causes of stress during a change process. Firstly, the unpredictability of change can generate anxiety, as individuals may not know what the future holds or how the change will impact their lives. Secondly, adapting to new circumstances can be overwhelming, triggering insecurity and anxiety, particularly if individuals feel ill-equipped to handle the new situation. Additionally, the loss of control that often accompanies change can be unsettling and contribute to stress. Furthermore, increased workloads resulting from the need to learn new skills, take on additional responsibilities, or deal with unexpected challenges can lead to feeling overwhelmed and heightened stress levels. Lastly, when change occurs within a social or professional context, the pressure to quickly adapt or conform to new norms can cause stress, especially if individuals feel they are not meeting new expectations. Understanding these causes of stress during a change process is essential, as it allows individuals to take proactive steps to mitigate stress and facilitate a smoother transition.

Navigating Uncertainty: Taking Risks and Embracing New Ideas

Leaders embrace new ideas as a strategic approach to navigating uncertainty because innovation and adaptability are essential for success in rapidly changing environments. With an openness to fresh ideas, resilient leaders create an environment that fosters creativity and imagination and encourages diverse perspectives, enabling them to stay ahead of the curve.

There are many upsides for underrepresented leaders in strategically taking risks. Firstly, taking calculated risks allow them to challenge the status quo and disrupt traditional norms. By introducing new approaches and ideas, underrepresented leaders can create opportunities for themselves and others, breaking through barriers and carving out their path to success.

Secondly, strategic risk-taking enables underrepresented leaders to differentiate themselves from leaders who operate within the status quo. They stand out in a crowded marketplace by embracing innovative ideas and pursuing unconventional strategies. This differentiation can lead to increased visibility, recognition, and growth.

Moreover, taking risks as an underrepresented leader is a powerful way to challenge biases and stereotypes. Resilient leaders demonstrate their capabilities and shatter preconceived notions by defying expectations and stepping outside prescribed roles. While doing so, the danger of the double bind of present and awareness of this risk must be factored into decision-making. This can inspire others facing similar challenges, opening doors and creating a more inclusive environment for future generations.

Additionally, embracing risk-taking leads to personal growth and development. Stepping out of one's comfort zone and facing uncertainty cultivate resilience, confidence, and adaptability. It provides opportunities for learning, experimentation, and acquiring new skills. These experiences strengthen underrepresented leaders, enabling them to overcome obstacles and navigate future challenges effectively.

Resilient leaders embrace new ideas to navigate uncertainty because they recognize the importance of innovation and adaptability. For underrepresented leaders, strategically taking risks offers several upsides, including challenging the status quo, differentiating themselves, challenging biases, and fostering personal growth. By being open to new possibilities and embracing calculated risks, underrepresented leaders can chart their own path to success and inspire others along the way.

Chemicals in the Brain

When individuals take risks in leadership, it sets in motion a fascinating interplay of neurochemical processes within the brain. As the decision-making centers and reward pathways come into play, various neurotransmitters and hormones activate, influencing their thoughts, emotions, and behaviors. The brain responds to career risks by releasing chemicals such as dopamine, which drives motivation and anticipation of rewards, and adrenaline, which heightens alertness and prepares the body for action. Understanding the neural mechanisms behind risk-taking in careers sheds light on the complex interplay between biology and behavior, highlighting the intricate processes that shape our professional journeys.

As the leader begins tapping into activities that call for resiliency, several chemicals are activated within the brain.

Dopamine, is the neurotransmitter associated with motivation, goal-directed behavior, and a sense of reward. When we experience success in the face of adversity, dopamine is released, helping us to feel positive and motivated to persist.

Serotonin is the neurotransmitter associated with mood regulation and well-being. When we feel in control of our lives and progress toward our goals, serotonin levels increase, helping us feel more optimistic and resilient.

Norepinephrine is the neurotransmitter associated with alertness and attention. When we need to be alert and focused in the face of adversity, norepinephrine levels increase, helping us to stay focused and on top of the situation.

Cortisol is the hormone associated with stress. While high levels of cortisol can be detrimental to our well-being in the long term, short-term increases in cortisol can help us to respond quickly and effectively to stressors, promoting resilience.

Oxytocin, this hormone is associated with social bonding and trust. When we have strong social support and feel connected to others, oxytocin levels increase, promoting feelings of security and resilience.

These chemicals are essential in promoting resilience by helping us stay motivated, focused, and optimistic in the face of adversity.

Leading Through Change: Inspiring Others to Embrace Transformation

Inspiring others to embrace transformation is a crucial aspect of leadership for underrepresented leaders in male-dominated industries. Here are some strategies to help you inspire others to embrace change:

Openly share your journey and experiences as an underrepresented leader. Highlight the challenges you've overcome and the lessons you've learned. By sharing your story, you humanize the change process and inspire others to believe in their ability to navigate transformation. Carla Harris is an example of an underrepresented leader who has successfully navigated the career jungle as a Black Woman in leadership on Wall Street.

Resilient Leader Profile: Carla Harris

Carla Harris is a well-respected Wall Street executive, accomplished gospel singer, and sought-after author who embodies personal and professional resilience. Her unique blend of talents and achievements has made her an inspiring figure for underrepresented leaders in the world of finance.

As a Wall Street executive, Carla has achieved decades-long success, delivering results to hit company objectives through the highs and lows of market conditions. She serves as Vice Chairman at Morgan Stanley and has held various leadership positions. Despite the challenges and competitive nature of the financial industry, Carla has consistently demonstrated resilience in navigating obstacles and achieving her goals, which she shares in her series of books and her keynote speeches.

Carla's resilience is rooted in her unwavering determination to be herself, even if it makes others uncomfortable. She is known for her relentless work ethic, always striving for excellence in everything she does by asking questions while in the midst of changing marketplace conditions. She has faced setbacks and adversity along her journey as a Black Woman on Wall Street, yet her ability to persevere and bounce back has been instrumental in her success.

Beyond her professional accomplishments, Carla's resilience shines through in her passion for gospel music. As a talented singer, she has captivated audiences with her powerful and soulful performances, including several sold-out performances at Carnegie Hall. Through music, Carla finds solace, inspiration, and a means to connect with others on a deeper level. Her ability to balance her corporate career with her artistic pursuits is a testament to her ability to boldly lean into her full set of skills and importance in nurturing her passions.

Carla's resilience extends to her role as an author and public speaker. She has authored several books, including *Expect to Win: 10 Proven Strategies for Thriving in the Workplace* and *Strategize to Win: The New Way to Start Out, Step Up, or Start Over in Your Career*. Carla shares her experiences, wisdom, and strategies for success through her writing and speaking engagements, empowering others to overcome challenges and embrace resilience in their own lives.

One of Carla's notable traits as a resilient leader is her ability to inspire and uplift those around her. She firmly believes in mentorship and actively advocates for diversity and inclusion in the workplace. Carla has dedicated her time and energy to empowering women and underrepresented individuals, providing guidance and support to help them overcome barriers and thrive in their careers.

Carla Harris exemplifies the qualities of a resilient leader. Her determination, tenacity, and adaptability to adversity have shaped her journey and inspired others. She is a powerful role model, demonstrating that one can overcome challenges and achieve greatness in multiple domains with resilience, passion, and a strong sense of purpose.

Nurturing Change on a Personal Level

A primary step in being resilient during moments of change is leading oneself. For leaders, however, this primary step is two-fold: you must also nurture team members to boost their resiliency for change. In the Resilient Leader's Program, we discuss ways to build strong relationships with our team members and colleagues by connecting to them on a personal level. This involves being intentional about understanding their aspirations, concerns, and motivations. As a result, you'll be able to show empathy and create a safe space for open dialogue. When your team members feel understood and supported, they are more likely to embrace change. Resilient leaders can connect personally without oversharing by following fundamental principles and incorporating insights from Brené Brown's research on vulnerability and connection.

Brené Brown is a renowned researcher, author, and public speaker known for her work on vulnerability, courage, empathy, and shame. She has spent over two decades studying topics related to human connection and emotions, and her insights have resonated with millions of people worldwide.

Brown's TED Talk, "The Power of Vulnerability," has been viewed millions of times and is one of the most-watched TED Talks ever. Her research emphasizes embracing vulnerability to foster authentic connections, cultivate resilience, and lead a more fulfilling life.

Brown has written several bestselling books, including *Daring Greatly*, *Rising Strong*, and *Braving the Wilderness*. Through her books, she explores themes such as shame, resilience, courage, wholehearted living, and the impact of vulnerability on personal and professional relationships.

Her work has profoundly influenced psychology, leadership, education, and self-development. Brown's teachings encourage individuals and leaders to embrace vulnerability, build empathy, and create environments that foster trust and connection. Through Brené Brown's work, leaders can delve deeper into the personal motivations for work to help them uncover mindset skills to nurture change within themselves and others.

Resilient Leader Strategies:

According to the *Oxford English Dictionary*, empathy is the ability to understand and share the feelings of another. Because of the variety of life experiences that someone brings into the workplace, there will be a varied response to accepting change. Empathy is crucial in building strong relationships with team members and colleagues as you guide your team while navigating the nuances of being an underrepresented leader. It involves demonstrating genuine care and understanding by putting yourself in their shoes, actively listening to their perspectives, and acknowledging their emotions and experiences.

As leaders guiding team members through change processes, it can be tempting to set an expectation that all people respond to changes in the same manner. While it would be easy for organizations to move from point A to Z with everyone responding the same way, it is unrealistic. People adapt to change at different rates and leaders who are emphatic are able to notice signs of resistance to change. The pressures of achieving KPIs (Key Performance Indicators) can blur the lines between being an empathic leader and one who gets results. However, research on the quiet quitting movement shows that employees who are seen, valued, and heard have a more positive mindset when navigating change. This recognition of the employee by the empathic leader helps the leader communicate directly with a potentially disengaged employee, thus interrupting quiet quitting before it begins. Empathy and resilience modeled in leadership help employees to remain engaged in work even in the process of change.

By showing empathy, resilient leaders create a foundation of trust that fosters connection and collaboration, allowing the team to adapt to change and move forward to achieve company goals. Understanding and valuing the thoughts and feelings of others helps establish an environment where people feel heard, seen, and supported. This, in turn, contributes to healthier communication, enhanced teamwork, and increased engagement among team members. Consider how you leverage empathy in your current leadership role. Are you conscious of its role in your decision-making?

You may be aware of these concepts, but in my experience, when there are competing priorities, leaders tend to react to the day's challenge and aren't putting these best practices into play. Resilient Leaders should be mindful of actively focusing on a conversation without interrupting or prematurely formulating a response. Furthermore, reflecting on the thoughts and feelings of your colleagues shows that you value their perspective and encourage them to share more openly. For instance, paraphrasing their statements or asking clarifying questions can convey that you are actively engaged and committed to understanding their point of view. By consistently practicing active listening, resilient leaders can foster deeper connections, enhance communication, and build trust within their teams, thus increasing empathy skills throughout your professional circle.

Chapter 2

CULTIVATING A GROWTH MINDSET: UNLOCKING YOUR POTENTIAL

Dear Resilient Leader,

I hope this email finds you well. In my last message to you, I talked about what it means to be a resilient leader, some of the obstacles we face, and some of the main ideas behind the Resilient Leaders Program. Today, I want to emphasize the importance of cultivating a growth mindset before embarking on this transformative journey.

At ZeroGap.co, we firmly believe that a growth mindset is the foundation for personal and professional development. It is a powerful tool that unlocks your potential and propels you toward achieving your goals. By adopting a growth mindset, you open yourself up to endless possibilities and embrace challenges as opportunities for growth.

The Resilient Leaders Program is designed to help you develop the skills and mindset necessary to navigate today's complex business landscape. It is a comprehensive program that equips you with the tools to overcome obstacles, lead with resilience, and thrive in times of uncertainty.

However, it is essential to recognize that the journey toward becoming a resilient leader starts within yourself. Cultivating a growth mindset lays the groundwork for personal transformation and sets the stage for continuous improvement. It allows you to approach challenges with curiosity, view failures as learning opportunities, and confidently adapt to change.

Throughout the Resilient Leaders Program, we delve deep into various aspects of leadership, including self-awareness, emotional intelligence, effective communication, and strategic decision-making. A growth mindset will serve as the lens through which you process and apply these learnings, allowing you to harness your full potential as a leader.

Please reflect on your current mindset and be open to embracing a growth-oriented perspective. As we embark on this journey together, remember that growth is a continuous process, and every step you take toward cultivating a growth mindset brings you closer to becoming the resilient leader you aspire to be.

Thank you for choosing the Resilient Leaders Program. I am confident that with your commitment to personal growth and our comprehensive training experience, you will achieve remarkable results. I look forward to witnessing your transformation and celebrating your success.

Wishing you an abundance of growth and resilience.

Warm regards,
Jacqueline V. Twillie
Founder of ZeroGap.co
Creator of the Resilient Leaders Program

The Power of a Growth Mindset: Embracing Setbacks and Failures

Growth Mindset

A growth mindset is a belief that one's abilities and intelligence can be developed through effort, perseverance, and learning. It is the opposite of a fixed mindset, which assumes that talents and qualities are innate and unchangeable. People with a growth mindset embrace challenges, view failure as an opportunity for growth, and believe in the power of continuous learning. This mindset fosters resilience, adaptability, and a willingness to take on new challenges.

Carol Dweck, a renowned psychologist and professor at Stanford University is widely recognized for her groundbreaking research on the concept of mindset. Dweck's work has focused on understanding how mindset influences individuals' motivation, performance, and personal development. She has extensively studied the impact of fixed and growth mindsets in various contexts, including education, sports, and the workplace. Through her research, Dweck has shown that individuals with a growth mindset achieve higher success and well-being.

Male-dominated industries often present unique challenges and barriers for women and underrepresented individuals, in part because social and legal systems have historically excluded these individuals from being in the workplace in a leadership capacity. There's no denying that the exclusionary history of these systems create very real barriers to success. Many of these obstacles may seem too great for us to face alone. With that said, the growth mindset can help us as individual leaders to transform some of these barriers into opportunities for development and empowerment. Instead of being discouraged or disheartened by discrimination, each experience can strengthen the skills, understanding, and resilience we need to overcome it.

Armed with the growth mindset, we don't only learn to conquer adversities individually. We also encourage others to seek innovative solutions, create inclusive and supportive environments, and empower those who work with us to contribute their unique perspectives. We place ourselves in the best position to foster diversity and challenge the very systems that once held some groups back. For these reasons, the growth mindset is essential to the R4 framework.

In the R4 framework, growth mindset development involves building self-awareness, identifying limiting beliefs, reframing negative self-talk, and cultivating a growth mindset through deliberate practice. Here are a few examples of how a growth mindset can be used to navigate challenges in the workplace:

Embracing Feedback: Rather than seeing feedback as criticism, a growth mindset allows leaders to view feedback as an opportunity to learn and improve. They use feedback to identify improvement areas and develop new skills and knowledge.

Embracing Failure: Leaders with a growth mindset don't see failure as the end of the road but as a valuable learning experience. They use their failures to learn, grow, and don't give up easily.

Seeking Challenges: Leaders with a growth mindset seek out challenges that will help them develop new skills and knowledge. They view challenges as opportunities to stretch their abilities and expand their capabilities.

Taking Risks: Leaders with a growth mindset are willing to take risks, knowing failure is possible. They see risks as opportunities to learn and grow and are ready to take calculated risks to achieve their goals.

Persistence: Leaders with a growth mindset don't give up easily. They persist in facing obstacles, knowing success often requires hard work and dedication. They view challenges as opportunities to develop grit and perseverance, essential for success in any field.

Resilient leaders exercise an unwavering commitment to their core values. They recognize that their values are a compass and allow this compass to guide their actions and leadership style. In this way, they also model accountability and reinforce their trustworthiness at every stage of the decision-making process. This marriage of a growth mindset and core values of accountability empowers leaders to navigate challenges with resilience, inspire their teams, and create a culture that upholds the highest standards of integrity and personal growth.

Continuous Learning and Development: Enhancing Your Skills and Abilities

Continuous learning and commitment to personal development are key advantages for resilient leaders. By actively seeking opportunities to enhance their skills and abilities, resilient leaders can stay ahead in a rapidly evolving world and effectively navigate challenges. Here are seven examples of how continuous learning and personal development can benefit leaders:

First, underrepresented leaders who leverage adaptability, innovation, and problem-solving as strategic advantages gain several benefits. Adaptability allows them to navigate the unique challenges and obstacles they may face in their respective industries. By quickly acquiring new knowledge and skills, they can effectively respond to evolving circumstances and adjust strategies and approaches accordingly. This adaptability enables underrepresented leaders to stay resilient, seize opportunities, and overcome barriers that may arise due to their backgrounds or circumstances.

Secondly, leveraging innovation as a strategic advantage allows underrepresented leaders to bring fresh ideas and perspectives. By actively seeking innovative solutions and staying updated on emerging trends, they can drive positive change within their teams and organizations. This mindset fosters creativity and helps underrepresented leaders find unique solutions to problems, enhancing competitiveness and growth.

Lastly, problem-solving skills play a crucial role in the success of underrepresented leaders. By committing to their own development, they acquire diverse problem-solving tools, enabling them to tackle complex challenges effectively. Drawing upon their varied knowledge and experiences, they can think vitally, explore multiple solutions, and find effective strategies to address obstacles and drive success.

Overall, underrepresented leaders who leverage adaptability, innovation, and problem-solving as strategic advantages gain a competitive edge in their industries. By embracing continuous learning and personal development, they can overcome barriers, drive innovation, and find creative solutions to complex problems, ultimately paving the way for their success and the success of their teams and organizations.

Underrepresented leaders can enhance their resilience to navigate market and societal challenges by focusing on emotional intelligence, strategic thinking, resilience modeling, and cross-functional collaboration. Emotional intelligence is crucial in building strong relationships, effective communication, and conflict resolution. Underrepresented leaders can navigate diverse environments, establish trust, and foster inclusive work cultures by investing in developing their interpersonal skills. For example, they can actively listen to the needs and perspectives of their team members, demonstrate empathy, and create an environment where everyone feels valued and supported.

To remain a competitive leader navigating industry trends, market dynamics, and organizational nuances, strategic thinking coupled with resiliency skills is essential for underrepresented leaders. Continuous learning enables them to expand their knowledge base and gain insights that inform informed decision-making and long-term planning. Underrepresented leaders can proactively adapt their strategies and seize opportunities by staying updated on market shifts and anticipating challenges. For instance, they can leverage data analytics to identify emerging trends or invest in technology to stay ahead of the curve in their respective industries.

Resilience modeling is a powerful tool for underrepresented leaders to inspire and motivate their teams. By prioritizing their personal development and embracing continuous learning, they set an example for their employees to follow. Through their actions, underrepresented leaders demonstrate the importance of growth mindsets, perseverance, and resilience in facing challenges. This modeling inspires their teams to embrace continuous learning, overcome obstacles, and pursue professional growth.

Cross-functional collaboration is vital for underrepresented leaders to bridge knowledge gaps and harness the diverse perspectives of their colleagues. They can effectively collaborate across different functions and departments by enhancing their skills in areas outside their core expertise, such as finance, marketing, or technology. This collaboration fosters innovation, creativity, and problem-solving, enabling underrepresented leaders to tackle complex challenges collectively. For example, they can lead cross-functional teams to develop comprehensive strategies that address market and societal challenges from multiple angles.

By leveraging emotional intelligence, strategic thinking, resilience modeling, and cross-functional collaboration, underrepresented leaders can enhance their resilience to navigate market and societal challenges. These skills enable them to build strong relationships, make informed decisions, inspire their teams, and collaborate effectively, ultimately leading to their success and driving positive change in their industries and communities.

Continuous learning and personal development are instrumental in cultivating resilient leaders who can expand their capabilities, maintain adaptability, and inspire their teams. Embracing a mindset of growth and investing in self-improvement allows leaders to drive innovation, effectively solve complex problems, and foster a culture of continuous learning within their organizations. By actively seeking opportunities for growth and staying updated on emerging knowledge and skills, resilient leaders are better equipped to navigate challenges and lead their teams toward success. Moreover, their commitment to personal development sets an inspiring example for others, encouraging a culture of continuous improvement and learning that leads to increased innovation and overall organizational growth.

From Limiting Beliefs to Limitless Potential: Overcoming Self-Doubt

Leaders can leverage a growth mindset to become adaptable to challenges and unleash their limitless potential. To shift from limiting beliefs to embracing a growth mindset, leaders can begin by acknowledging and challenging their self-doubt and imposter syndrome. By recognizing that these feelings are common and not indicative of their true abilities, leaders can take proactive steps to overcome them.

One effective strategy is to focus on evidence-based thinking. Leaders can gather evidence of their past achievements and successes, reminding themselves of their capabilities and accomplishments. This practice helps counteract self-doubt and reinforces a positive self-perception. Additionally, seeking support from mentors, coaches, or trusted colleagues can provide valuable perspectives and guidance, helping leaders gain confidence in their abilities and challenge imposter syndrome.

Another helpful approach is reframing failure as a learning opportunity. Embracing a growth mindset means viewing setbacks as stepping stones to growth and improvement. Leaders can reframe failures as valuable experiences that provide lessons and insights for future success. By adopting a curious and reflective mindset, leaders can extract valuable learnings from challenges and use them as catalysts for personal and professional growth.

High-performance leaders in various fields, such as Serena Williams in sports, provide valuable insights and hacks for success. One common trait among these leaders is their ability to embrace a growth mindset and continuously strive for improvement. They focus on deliberate practice, setting specific goals, and consistently pushing their boundaries to enhance their skills and abilities.

Additionally, high-performance leaders understand the importance of mental and physical well-being. They prioritize self-care, including regular exercise, proper nutrition, and adequate rest, recognizing that a healthy mind and body are essential for sustained high performance. They also seek feedback and actively solicit input from trusted advisors, recognizing that continuous learning and seeking external perspectives contribute to their growth and success.

Leaders can use a growth mindset to become adaptable to challenges and tap into their limitless potential. Overcoming self-doubt and imposter syndrome involves challenging limiting beliefs, focusing on evidence-based thinking, reframing failure as an opportunity for growth, and seeking support from mentors and peers. By adopting strategies inspired by high-performance leaders like Serena Williams, such as deliberate practice, prioritizing well-being, and seeking feedback, leaders can unlock their full potential and achieve exceptional results in their personal and professional lives.

Resilient Leader Profile: Serena Williams

Serena Williams, a true icon in the world of tennis, embodies the qualities of a resilient leader as she transitions from the tennis court to venture capitalism. Beyond her extraordinary athletic achievements, Serena's focus on her mindset for personal growth sets her apart as an exceptional leader. She has consistently demonstrated a growth mindset throughout her career, embracing challenges and seeking personal and professional development opportunities.

Serena Williams recognizes that mindset plays a vital role in achieving success. She understands the importance of resilience and perseverance in facing setbacks and obstacles. Serena's growth mindset enables her to view failures as learning experiences and motivates her to improve her skills persistently. By maintaining a positive and resilient attitude, she has been able to bounce back from adversity and maintain her competitive edge.

In her transition to venture capitalism, Serena's growth mindset continues to drive her pursuit of personal growth. She has expanded her knowledge and expertise by immersing herself in business and actively seeking opportunities to learn and grow. Serena embraces the challenges of venturing into a new industry, recognizing that the skills and mindset that propelled her to greatness in tennis can also be applied to her entrepreneurial endeavors.

Serena's growth mindset extends beyond personal growth; she is passionate about empowering others to develop their full potential. Through her investments and partnerships, she supports and uplifts entrepreneurs, particularly those from underrepresented communities. Serena believes in the power of providing opportunities and resources to individuals who may face systemic barriers, reflecting her commitment to fostering inclusivity and diversity within the business world.

Serena Williams exemplifies a resilient leader who harnesses the power of a growth mindset for personal growth. Her unwavering determination, adaptability, and commitment to continuous learning have propelled her to great heights in the world of tennis and successfully enabled her to navigate new ventures, such as venture capitalism. Serena's focus on mindset serves as an inspiration to aspiring leaders, reminding them of the importance of resilience, personal development, and creating opportunities for others.

Chapter 3

FOSTERING COLLABORATION: BUILDING INCLUSIVE AND SUPPORTIVE ENVIRONMENTS

Dear Resilient Leader,

I hope this email finds you in good health and high spirits. As one leader to another, it is my absolute pleasure to connect with you as we each continue our journey to become catalysts for positive change in our professional spheres. Today, I wanted to share some insights about fostering collaboration. There are two dimensions of collaboration that we see at play in the workplace: the day-to-day interactions between our team members and, in a broader sense, the culture we create in our organizations. On both the interpersonal and organizational levels, each of us can cultivate a work experience for ourselves and our colleagues that is filled with joy and abundance.

Why exactly is fostering collaboration crucial in today's professional landscape? In a rapidly changing world, organizations that encourage teamwork, cooperation, and diverse perspectives are the most likely to succeed. They are better equipped to navigate challenges, spark innovation, and achieve exceptional results. Collaboration is the guiding principle that will bring together the tapestry of unique talents, experiences, and ideas that your organization needs in order to thrive. Furthermore, it will make the difference between being a leader who gains short-term results and one who empowers your entire network to achieve long-ranging, lifelong success.

Building an inclusive and supportive environment is a vital aspect of collaboration. It entails creating spaces where everyone's voice is heard, and diverse perspectives are not only accepted but celebrated. When individuals from different backgrounds, genders, ethnicities, and abilities come together in a space that values their contributions, the potential for growth and success becomes limitless. Moreover, an inclusive workplace engenders a sense of psychological safety, enabling employees to bring their authentic selves to work and unlocking their full potential.

Now, let's delve into strategies and actionable steps to foster collaboration and build inclusive and supportive environments:

Lead by Example: *As a resilient leader, your actions set the tone for the entire team. Embrace inclusivity, actively seek diverse perspectives, and create opportunities for collaboration. Encourage open and honest communication and demonstrate empathy and respect in all interactions.*

Foster Psychological Safety: *Cultivate an environment where team members feel safe to take risks, make mistakes, and share their opinions without fear of retribution. Encourage open dialogue, active listening, and constructive feedback.*

Promote Diversity and Inclusion: *Create policies and practices that promote diversity and inclusivity at all levels of the organization. Implement inclusive hiring processes, provide diversity and bias training, and establish mentorship and sponsorship programs that support underrepresented employees.*

Establish Collaborative Workspaces: *Design physical and virtual workspaces that facilitate collaboration. Foster cross-functional teams, encourage knowledge-sharing and promote collaboration through technology platforms and tools.*

Celebrate Achievements and Milestones: *Recognize and celebrate individual and team achievements. Acknowledge the unique contributions of each team member and create a culture of appreciation and gratitude.*

Remember, creating a thriving workplace requires ongoing commitment and continuous improvement. Together, we can pave the way for a future where diversity, collaboration, and inclusivity are the foundation of success.

Thank you for your time and dedication to fostering collaboration and supporting your team members. I look forward to hearing from you soon.

With warm regards,

Jacqueline V Twillie,
Founder of ZeroGap.co
Creator of the Resilient Leaders Program

Resilient leaders have historically leaned on one another to foster collaboration in tangible ways. They have done so to share resources, exchange knowledge, and learn from each other's experiences. The following are three common examples of how resilient leaders can leverage their community:

Networking and Mentoring: Resilient leaders can actively engage in networking and mentoring relationships with their peers and allies. By connecting with other leaders who share similar values and goals, they can exchange insights, advice, and best practices. Mentoring relationships provide opportunities for learning from experienced leaders, while networking allows for the exchange of ideas and collaboration on projects or initiatives. For example, a resilient leader may join professional associations or attend industry conferences to connect with like-minded individuals who can offer support and collaboration.

Collaboration Platforms and Communities: Resilient leaders can participate in collaboration platforms and communities that facilitate knowledge sharing and problem-solving. These platforms can be online forums, industry-specific groups, or even internal collaboration tools within organizations. By actively participating in these platforms, leaders can contribute their expertise, seek advice from others, and foster collaborative projects. For instance, resilient leaders may join an online community focused on diversity and inclusion in the workplace, where they can share insights and learn from others' experiences.

Cross-Organizational Initiatives: Resilient leaders can collaborate on cross-organizational initiatives that address common challenges or opportunities. Leaders can achieve greater impact and influence by pooling their resources, expertise, and networks. They can form partnerships or alliances to tackle industry-wide issues, drive policy changes, or promote diversity and inclusion initiatives. For example, leaders in the tech industry might join forces to address gender disparities in the field by creating mentorship programs, advocating for inclusive hiring practices, or establishing diversity and inclusion guidelines.

Being an inclusive and supportive community member involves actively contributing to and benefiting from collective efforts. This includes but isn't limited to how leaders can engage to navigate challenges and celebrate milestones within such a community:

Resilient leaders actively engage in sharing best practices, offering support and guidance, collaborating on projects, celebrating diversity and inclusion, and providing resources and opportunities within their community. They openly share their knowledge, lessons learned, and success stories, promoting the improvement of leadership practices in the community. By sharing their experiences, resilient leaders contribute to the growth and development of others, helping them learn and grow.

Collaborative projects are another avenue for resilient leaders to contribute to their communities. They initiate joint initiatives, research studies, or advocacy campaigns that bring together the collective expertise and resources of the community. By collaborating on projects that address common goals, leaders create meaningful change and make a lasting impact on their community.

Furthermore, resilient leaders actively promote and celebrate diversity and inclusion within their community. They encourage diverse perspectives, create safe spaces for dialogue, and recognize the achievements of underrepresented individuals. By fostering an inclusive environment, leaders contribute to their community's well-being and success.

Resilient leaders also leverage their networks, influence, and resources to provide opportunities for community members. They share job openings, recommend talented individuals for leadership positions, and connect community members with relevant resources or funding opportunities.

By actively supporting the growth and success of others, leaders contribute to building a stronger and more resilient community.

Resilient leaders play a crucial role in their community by sharing best practices, offering support and guidance, collaborating on projects, celebrating diversity and inclusion, and providing resources and opportunities. Their active engagement and contributions create an environment that fosters growth, collaboration, and success for all community members.

The 5 Strengths of Collaboration: Embracing Unique Talents and Perspectives

1. Cultural awareness (or cultural recognition) is the first strength we should discuss, given that a leader in today's society will encounter customers, clients, colleagues, and partners from many different backgrounds. Cultural recognition is the ability to understand the value of other cultures and also be aware of one's own culture. This involves being sensitive to how one's own upbringing influences our decisions as leaders, the distinctive attributes other people bring to the work dynamic, and how different cultural perspectives can work in unison. Developing this skill will take time, especially since we are always meeting new people. Nonetheless, honing this skill is well worth the effort.

   Resilient leaders who embrace cultural recognition understand the value that diverse perspectives and backgrounds bring to their teams. They leverage their knowledge of various cultures to bridge gaps and transform ideas that may initially be overlooked. They create an inclusive environment that fosters innovation and drives success by embracing and celebrating cultural diversity.

2. Meaningful communication is a strength of resilient leaders. Everyone communicates on some level; what distinguishes meaningful communication is the ability to truly connect with others. This requires listening to your audience or team, observing what they value, and developing an understanding of what they will be receptive to. Leaders who possess these communication skills can convey their ideas, visions, and goals in a way that resonates with others. Rather than just transmitting orders or information, their communication channels invoke meaning. Communication that is meaningful to team members inspires them to actively engage and contribute. Effective communication establishes a shared understanding and a sense of purpose among participants, promoting unity and collaboration.

3. Adaptability and inclusivity are essential strengths of resilient leaders who value collaboration. They recognize the importance of considering the needs and perspectives of all parties involved, even those not directly present in decision-making processes. They create a collaborative environment that harnesses the team's collective wisdom by actively seeking diverse viewpoints and ensuring everyone feels heard and included. This adaptability and inclusivity enable them to navigate complex challenges with agility and make decisions that benefit the entire organization or community.

4. Resilient leaders also possess a holistic perspective, allowing them to view both short-term and long-term stances. They understand the significance of balancing immediate objectives with long-term goals and sustainability. By considering the broader impact of their decisions and actions, they make informed choices that lead to positive outcomes. This comprehensive view enables them to guide their teams toward long-term success while addressing immediate needs effectively.

5. Another strength of resilient leaders is their ability to leverage individuals' unique talents and strengths within their teams. They recognize each team member's value and encourage them to contribute their expertise and ideas. Part of this strength involves paying attention to attributes in other people that may be overlooked by others. By valuing and utilizing these diverse skill sets, they foster an environment of creativity and high performance. This collaborative approach empowers team members to innovate, drive progress, and achieve common goals.

Unapologetic Leadership

The Essence of Unapologetic Leadership

Unapologetic leadership is rooted in embracing one's unique identity and experiences rather than seeking validation from others or conforming to the dominant social narratives about who we ought to be. It involves embracing authenticity, speaking up for oneself and others, and challenging systemic biases. Unapologetic leaders acknowledge their worth, recognize their potential, and harness their strengths to effect change.

Defining the "Other"

The term "other" refers to individuals who exist outside the dominant group or societal norms, whether due to race, gender, ethnicity, religion, sexual orientation, or any other characteristic that sets them apart. Being an "other" often means facing prejudice, discrimination, and limited opportunities. However, unapologetic leadership can emerge as a powerful force for transformation at this intersection.

Navigating the Intersection of Being an "Other"

Leaders from historically marginalized groups who occupy top leadership roles often navigate a unique intersection of challenges. We might be the only member of our group in a particular space. Colleagues or superiors from a dominant group might make decisions based on their biases while assuming those biases to be true. Practically speaking, this means they might be closed-minded when confronted with different ideas, perspectives, experiences, and styles. Our competence or capabilities might be questioned. Our very presence may even be questioned. In such an environment, they may look at you as the outsider or "other." Those who are made to feel like the Other because of their culture, sex, gender, race, ability, or appearance face a myriad of obstacles and biases that can hinder their progress. However, embracing unapologetic leadership can empower them to overcome adversity, redefine norms, and drive meaningful change.

Challenges Faced by "Others" in Leadership

Leaders who identify as "others" encounter numerous obstacles to success. They may face colleagues or higher-ups who impose stereotypes based on biased perceptions of your group. Your group may have very little representation in decision-making positions, which means you could be the only person in the room defending your perspective on important issues. You may experience impostor syndrome, which is the feeling that you don't belong or aren't qualified to hold your position—even though you worked hard to get where you are. You might feel this way because you are in an institution or organization that wasn't originally set up to embrace diversity, or as a result of hostile behaviors coming from coworkers. These hostile behaviors can be overt or subtle. The more subtle acts of hostility are often referred to as microaggressions. In general, microaggressions take place when someone singles you out for criticism, scrutiny, or closed-minded comments without using openly bigoted language.

Altogether, these various obstacles make it nearly impossible for members of underrepresented groups to reach certain executive positions, even when they are amply qualified. Since few organizations or businesses want to appear discriminatory, most will pay lip service to the ideals of diversity in their public-facing literature and statements. You have probably seen this at various points in your career. Nevertheless, the combined challenges listed above effectively prevent underrepresented people from reaching the highest levels in an industry or organization. This is why we often refer to this phenomenon as the glass ceiling or invisible ceiling effect. Although the challenges underrepresented leaders face in the professional world may be invisible from the outside, we know they are very real. These barriers can often make it difficult for "othered" people to navigate the workplace freely, build support networks, and gain equal opportunities for growth and advancement.

Resilient Leader Intersectional Strategies

To navigate the intersection of being seen as an "other," resilient leaders continue to embrace an unapologetic mindset. Embracing authenticity is a powerful trait that sets unapologetic leaders apart. By staying true to themselves, they demonstrate a deep sense of self-awareness and confidence in their values, beliefs, and experiences. This authenticity resonates with others, inspiring trust and admiration. When leaders are genuine and transparent, it creates an environment where individuals feel safe to express their true selves without fear of judgment or discrimination. By embracing their identities, unapologetic leaders encourage others to do the same, fostering a culture of inclusivity and acceptance. Their authenticity sends a powerful message that diversity is acknowledged and celebrated and that everyone's unique perspective has value. This enables individuals to bring their whole selves to the table, unlocking untapped potential and fueling collective growth and innovation.

Unapologetic leaders are not afraid to address bias and stereotypes directly. They recognize these harmful biases exist within individuals, organizations, and society at large. They take proactive steps to challenge and dismantle these biases, orchestrating a more inclusive environment for everyone involved. They engage in open and honest conversations about privilege, discrimination, and unconscious bias, creating spaces where people feel safe to share their experiences and perspectives.

These leaders also prioritize education and awareness as crucial tools in combating bias and stereotypes. They actively seek opportunities to educate themselves and others through workshops, training programs, or guest speakers. They encourage dialogue that challenges preconceived notions and encourages critical thinking. By educating others about the impact of biases and stereotypes, unapologetic leaders help individuals develop a greater understanding and empathy, fostering an environment of respect and acceptance.

One example of a leader challenging bias and stereotypes is Malala Yousafzai, the youngest Nobel Peace Prize laureate. As an advocate for girls' education and women's rights, Malala confronts the stereotypes that limit opportunities for girls and women. She fearlessly speaks out against discrimination, challenging societal norms and advocating for equal access to education. By leveraging her platform and sharing her story, Malala inspires others to challenge bias and work towards a more equitable world.

Another example is the #MeToo movement, which was ignited by courageous individuals speaking out against sexual harassment and assault. These brave individuals confronted a culture of silence and victim-blaming that is deeply entrenched in our society. By sharing their stories and starting difficult conversations, they sparked a global movement that shed light on the pervasive nature of sexual misconduct and forced a reckoning in various industries. Their steadfastness led to policy changes and increased awareness about the importance of consent and respect.

In both cases, unapologetic leaders recognize their desire to challenge bias and stereotypes head-on. They create platforms for discussion, education, and change. Their efforts give birth to inclusive environments where individuals can thrive regardless of race, gender, or background. By confronting bias and stereotypes, these leaders promote a more just and equitable society that benefits everyone.

Resilient leaders who adapt and lead by example possess an unapologetic mindset that guides their actions. They demonstrate integrity, empathy, and inclusivity in their leadership approach. By modeling the behaviors they expect from others, they create a powerful ripple effect that incites others to practice respect, fairness, and open dialogue. These leaders embody their values, consistently acting authentically and transparently. Their unwavering commitment to ethical conduct and empathy towards others inspires trust and encourages individuals to follow suit.

It is important to consider that there are many advantages and disadvantages to being on the vanguard of systemic change. On the positive side, changemakers often find a profound sense of purpose and fulfillment in their work. By challenging inequality and advocating for diversity, equity, and inclusion, they derive a deep sense of meaning from their efforts, contributing to their overall mental well-being. Their resilience and coping skills also play a crucial role. These leaders have developed strategies to navigate challenges and setbacks, allowing them to bounce back from adversity. Such resilience helps them maintain mental health while confronting systemic issues and facing resistance.

Furthermore, leaders driving systemic change often build support networks and find allies who share their vision. These connections provide emotional support and solidarity, allowing leaders to lean on others during difficult times. Such support reduces the impact on their mental health, offering a sense of belonging and reassurance.

However, some challenges can affect the mental health of resilient leaders. The process of driving systemic change can be taxing to the mind, body, and spirit. Constantly challenging organizational structures requires significant emotional energy, which can lead to exhaustion and burnout if not managed effectively. Additionally, these leaders may face resistance, backlash, or pushback from individuals or institutions invested in maintaining the status quo. Dealing with criticism, opposition, or hostility can affect their mental well-being, particularly when it is sustained over time.

Moreover, unapologetic leaders often hear and engage with the stories and experiences of marginalized individuals who have faced discrimination and inequality. This exposure to others' pain and suffering can weigh heavily on their mental health, leading to compassion fatigue or vicarious trauma if proper self-care practices are not in place.

To mitigate these challenges, it is essential for resilient leaders driving systemic change to prioritize self-care, establish boundaries, and seek support when needed. Engaging in activities that promote mental well-being, such as practicing self-reflection, seeking therapy or counseling, and connecting with supportive communities, can help leaders maintain their mental health while working towards meaningful and impactful change. By caring for their own well-being, they can continue to drive systemic change effectively and sustainably.

Benefits of Unapologetic Leadership

Unapologetic leadership offers several benefits to organizations, communities, and society.

Innovation and Creativity: Embracing diverse perspectives leads to innovative solutions and creative problem-solving. Unapologetic leaders bring fresh insights that can revolutionize industries and drive positive change.

Enhanced Employee Engagement: Inclusive leadership fosters employees' sense of belonging and engagement. When individuals feel valued and respected, they are likely to contribute their best work, increasing productivity and organizational success.

Empowerment of Others: Unapologetic leaders inspire and empower those who feel marginalized. By breaking down barriers, they create opportunities for others to thrive and reach their full potential.

Social Impact: Unapologetic leaders become catalysts for societal change. Challenging norms, addressing systemic inequities, and advocating for underrepresented groups create a fairer and more inclusive world.

Unapologetic leadership at the intersection of being an "other" holds immense power to transform organizations, communities, and society. By embracing authenticity, challenging biases, and driving systemic change, these leaders navigate their unique journeys with strength and resilience. As we strive for a more inclusive world, unapologetic leadership will guide others to embrace their identities and break down barriers for future generations.

Owning the Power of Being An Underrepresented Leader: Creativity and Cultural Celebration

Working in a male-dominated industry as an underrepresented leader can be challenging and empowering. This guide aims to help you confidently navigate such environments, leveraging your unique strengths, embracing creativity, embracing joy, and celebrating your cultural identity. By owning your power and using it to effect positive change, you can become an influential leader and inspire others to do the same. Let's explore some strategies and practical tips to help you succeed.

Embrace Your Authenticity

Recognize the immense value in your unique perspective and experiences as an underrepresented leader in a male-dominated industry. Your diverse background holds the potential to bring fresh ideas and innovative solutions to the table. Your distinct viewpoint is a powerful asset in the struggle to challenge the status quo, break through barriers, and inspire transformative change.

To create a better world, staying true to yourself and preserving your authenticity is vital. Resist the pressures to conform to the norms and leadership styles typically associated with white males for the sake of doing things as they've always been done. You don't have to become somebody else to be successful. Trying to do so will probably have the opposite effect. Regardless of the pressures to conform you may encounter in the world, being yourself is the surest path to long-term success. I want to be clear that numerous white male leaders exhibit leadership qualities that I admire and emulate, so this is not a statement to say all white male leaders are ineffective. Instead, my goal is to emphasize that there are many types of leaders beyond the narrow category of people who have dominated the Western workplace for decades.

It is important never to stifle or silence your authentic voice. Instead, use your cultural heritage to your advantage in your leadership journey. Everyone has a heritage and a culture; your willingness to embrace yours gives you insight into the people around you. It enables you to emphasize the importance of inclusion and understanding. It deepens the impact of your communication style. It gives you an interpersonal fluency that enables you to resolve misunderstandings, bridge knowledge gaps, encourage empathy, and establish meaningful connections with colleagues and stakeholders. When you are a leader who is proud of your cultural identity, your impact can go far beyond the walls and offices of your organization. You are setting an example for the kind of world you want to inhabit and the kind of practices that ought to define the workplace of the future.

In many ways, pride in your heritage and cultural perspective begins with having confidence in yourself as an individual. You are a representation of the people who invested in the future you now occupy. Everything you do is a continuation of their efforts. Remember your accomplishments and the skills that have propelled you to where you are today. One effective strategy to boost your confidence and keep track of your achievements is to create what I call a brag folder. I discuss this concept in my book *Navigating the Career Jungle: A Guide for Young Professionals.* A brag folder is a digital folder on your personal computer where you compile references to your notable work, awards, accolades, and other successes.

A brag folder is a valuable resource for leaders, allowing you to reflect on your achievements and contributions. It is a collection of evidence that showcases your capabilities, talents, and progress throughout your career. Whenever you need a confidence boost, you can refer to your brag folder as a reminder of your abilities and impact. This practice also equips you with concrete examples to share during performance reviews, interviews, negotiations, or when you are pursuing new opportunities.

Start your brag folder today and regularly update it with your professional milestones. Capture positive feedback, testimonials, notable projects, certifications, and any recognition you receive. As you continue to build your career, your brag folder will become a valuable tool for self-assurance and a testament to your growth and accomplishments. Believe in yourself and leverage the power of your achievements as you navigate and excel in male-dominated industries.

Embracing Joy: The Path to Authenticity and Cultural Celebration in Resilient Leadership

We all understand that resilient leaders can adapt, bounce back from setbacks, and lead their teams through challenging times. However, amidst the pressures of leadership, these individuals need to remember the importance of joy and abundance in their professional lives.

Resilient leaders understand that prioritizing joy not only benefits their well-being but also enhances their effectiveness.

One of the key benefits of prioritizing joy is the ability to be more forthright in leadership. When leaders allow themselves to experience and express joy, they tap into their true selves, enabling them to lead from a place of authenticity. Authenticity fosters trust and connection within teams, allowing others to see their leader's genuine character. With someone with forthrightness and integrity at the helm, team members will be more receptive to new initiatives, policy changes, and endeavors that may require an element of sacrifice or risk. A leader's enthusiastic belief in themselves will give the dreams they believe in greater credibility in the eyes of those they lead.

Moreover, joy reinforces resilience. In times of adversity and stress, experiencing joy can help leaders maintain a positive mindset and navigate challenges with greater ease. By infusing joy into their leadership style, resilient leaders bring a sense of lightness and optimism to their teams, promoting a culture of resilience and perseverance. They create an atmosphere where obstacles are seen as opportunities for growth rather than insurmountable barriers.

Embracing joy and abundance allows resilient leaders to celebrate their culture, especially in workspaces where they may be among the few representing their heritage. In such environments, it is crucial to establish a sense of cultural inclusivity and appreciation. By prioritizing joy, resilient leaders can infuse their unique cultural perspectives into the workplace, fostering diversity and creating an environment where everyone feels valued.

So, how can resilient leaders prioritize joy and abundance in how they show up at work? Here are a few strategies to consider:

1. **Embrace gratitude:** Daily gratitude helps resilient leaders appreciate the present moment and find joy in even the smallest accomplishments. Encourage your team to join you in expressing gratitude, fostering a culture of appreciation.

2. **Incorporate playfulness:** Infuse moments of playfulness and fun into work routines. This can range from team-building activities to celebrating milestones with light-hearted games or events. By embracing playfulness, resilient leaders create a sense of joy and camaraderie within their teams.

3. **Lead by example:** Resilient leaders should actively model the behavior they wish to see in their teams. By demonstrating their joy and celebrating their culture, they encourage others to do the same, fostering a workplace where everyone feels empowered to embrace their identities.

4. **Encourage self-care:** Prioritizing joy and abundance requires caring for oneself. Resilient leaders should emphasize the importance of self-care to their teams and provide support and resources to promote work-life balance and overall well-being.

Tell Stories with Pride

There are narratives embedded in every area of life and every form of communication. Every time you introduce yourself, reinforce an existing rule, set a new policy, outline a budget, advocate a change, or articulate a plan for the future, you tell a story. You tell a story about who you are as a leader or collectively as a team. This is why the most effective leaders are often great storytellers. Storytelling techniques can effectively convey your experiences and make your messages more relatable. By sharing stories rooted in personal experience or conviction, you can help others understand your challenges and the unique opportunities that arise from diversity. Furthermore, by framing your story in terms of abundance, advancement, achievement, or joy, you cause others to want to join it.

Craft compelling narratives highlighting your journey, showcasing the hurdles you've overcome and the lessons you've learned along the way. Illustrate the value of diversity by weaving in anecdotes demonstrating its positive impact on your work and the organization. By sharing your experiences through storytelling, you can humanize struggles and triumphs, thereby promoting empathy and understanding among your colleagues.

Very few people are expert storytellers from the start. Like many skills, crafting compelling narratives takes time to perfect. There are, however, some basic tips that, if employed, will give you a solid foundation. For instance, tap into the emotions and experiences that shape your unique perspective. Use vivid language and imagery to paint a picture that captivates your audience. This approach engages others deeper and helps them relate to your story, drawing connections to their experiences. These sorts of techniques make the difference between you communicating abstract concepts or ideas that can truly influence the hearts and minds of other people. Before long, you will see how central conscious storytelling is to maintaining a spirit of collaboration in your place of work.

Resilient Leader Profile: Shonda Rhimes - Masterful Storyteller and Trailblazing Producer

In dynamic storytelling, few names shine as brightly as Shonda Rhimes. A visionary leader, Rhimes has revolutionized television with her captivating narratives. She left an indelible mark on the entertainment industry as one of the first major producers to secure a groundbreaking deal with Netflix in 2017, catapulting her already successful career to new heights. With an unparalleled ability to weave intricate tales that resonate with audiences worldwide, Rhimes has become an emblematic figure of resilience, storytelling, and innovation.

Throughout her journey as a leader within the entertainment industry, Rhimes has consistently defied conventions and shattered barriers, which is evident in her record-breaking statistics on many shows. Born and raised in Chicago, she discovered her passion for storytelling at a young age, immersing herself in books, plays, and films that sparked her imagination. Her innate talent for crafting compelling narratives blossomed at Dartmouth College and later at the University of Southern California's School of Cinematic Arts, where she honed her skills and laid the foundation for her future success.

Rhimes burst onto the scene in the early 2000s, captivating audiences with her groundbreaking medical drama series, "Grey's Anatomy." With its diverse cast, complex characters, and gripping storylines, the show quickly became a cultural phenomenon, drawing millions of viewers week after week. Rhimes fearlessly explored sensitive topics, delving into the complexities of human relationships, the fragility of life, and the resilience of the human spirit. Her ability to tackle challenging subjects with authenticity and empathy established her as a trailblazer in the television landscape. She's been vocal about her unapologetic views of writing for female main characters working in male-dominated industries.

As her career soared, Rhimes continued to push boundaries and challenge industry norms. In 2007, she introduced another groundbreaking series, "Private Practice," delving into the intricacies of the medical profession from a fresh perspective. The show's success further solidified Rhimes' reputation as a dynamic storyteller with a knack for capturing the essence of human emotions and experiences.

In 2017, Rhimes again made headlines by securing an unprecedented deal with streaming giant Netflix. This landmark agreement, worth over

$100 million, showcased her remarkable ability to adapt and embrace new platforms, cementing her status as a visionary producer unafraid to embrace change. Rhimes embarked on a new chapter with this partnership, bringing her unparalleled storytelling prowess to a global audience hungry for innovative and diverse narratives.

Beyond her professional achievements, Rhimes also embodies resilience in her personal life. As an African-American woman in a predominantly white and male industry, she has confronted and overcome numerous challenges, blazing a trail for aspiring storytellers from underrepresented communities. By fearlessly amplifying diverse voices and championing inclusive storytelling, Rhimes has become a powerful advocate for underrepresented groups, opening doors and paving the way for greater representation and authenticity in the entertainment industry.

Shonda Rhimes' journey is a testament to the transformative power of resilience and unwavering determination. Her ability to captivate audiences with her storytelling and her trailblazing deal with Netflix showcases her profound impact on the entertainment world. As a resilient leader, Rhimes continues to inspire countless individuals, reminding us that our dreams are within reach if we dare to push boundaries, embrace change, and unleash the power of our unique narratives upon the world.

Understand Different Perspectives

Let's consider an example of how to practice active listening and engage in constructive dialogue to understand different perspectives and foster collaboration. Imagine you are leading a team meeting in a male-dominated industry, discussing a new project proposal. As the conversation unfolds, it becomes apparent that your team members hold varying opinions and perspectives. To practice active listening and foster collaboration, follow these steps:

1. Create an inclusive environment by setting the tone for open and respectful communication. Emphasize that all viewpoints are valuable, encouraging team members to express their thoughts freely and without judgment.

2. Listen attentively to each team member's contributions. Give them your undivided attention, demonstrating your engagement through eye contact and non-verbal cues. By actively listening, you show respect for their ideas and opinions.

3. Ask clarifying questions to gain a deeper understanding of their perspective. Thoughtful inquiries encourage speakers to elaborate, enabling you to grasp the nuances and complexities of their viewpoints. This approach demonstrates your genuine interest in comprehending their position.

4. Reflect and paraphrase their key points after each team member shares their perspective. Summarizing their thoughts ensures your understanding and communicates that you value their input. This allows speakers to correct any misunderstandings and further enriches the dialogue.

5. In pursuing collaboration, seek common ground among the different perspectives. Identify areas of agreement or shared goals, highlighting these commonalities to bridge gaps and foster rapport. By focusing on shared interests, you can cultivate an environment of collaboration and teamwork.

6. Encourage constructive dialogue within the team. Create a space where members feel comfortable respectfully challenging ideas and offering alternative solutions. Maintain a focus on the topic to ensure productive and relevant discussions.

7. Facilitate the search for consensus among team members. Guide the conversation to find common ground and reach an agreement.

Encourage exploration of compromises and consideration of different perspectives, ultimately working towards the best possible outcome.

These steps will help you build a stronger team, one that is able to fully harness the innovation, diversity, intellectual power, and collaborative ability that exists among its members.

Resilient Leader Strategy: Cultivating Creativity

To harness your team's creativity as a resilient leader in a male-dominated industry, follow these steps:

1. Make the most of your ability to think outside the box. Utilize your unique perspective to identify untapped opportunities, develop creative solutions, or challenge conventional norms that aren't serving your mission or the interests of your team.

2. Encourage your team members to provide constructive criticism about a policy or practice and the workplace. Sometimes, innovating new and better ideas begins with asking your colleagues what isn't working.

3. Highlight the ideas of team members who tend to play a supportive role in your team's operations. The thing about diversity is that it is not a finite resource. There are underrepresented voices, even among underrepresented groups of people. There is always someone who has something more to offer. Introducing some seldom-heard voices into a conversation can spark innovative outcomes.

4. Encourage brainstorming sessions and experimentation, allowing room for unconventional ideas and approaches.

Every time a leader enables something new into the workplace dynamic—whether that be a new idea, a new voice, or a new opportunity to look at things from a different perspective—you renew the creative power that is housed within the members of your team. Do this whenever you can, and you will experience more positive outcomes.

Celebrate Cultural Heritage

Aside from voicing support for diversity and inclusion initiatives in theory, what can be done practically? The following are some ideas to make you advocate diversity in both word and deed.

1. Embrace and celebrate your cultural heritage in the workplace by sharing traditions, festivals, and customs with your colleagues. Sharing one's culture can be a frightening idea for people who are more used to workplaces that impose conformity. By demonstrating the courage to express your culture openly, you invite your team members to do the same.

2. Actively promote diversity and inclusion initiatives within your organization. New DEI initiatives in a workplace do not catch on immediately, especially among colleagues who are wary of policy changes. Vocal supporters can turn the tide towards embracing progress. If you champion these efforts, you help to create a more equitable workplace for everyone.

3. Besides supporting DEI efforts launched by others, you can create new ones yourself. Use every bit of authority or leverage you have in the workplace to organize events or initiatives that highlight different cultures or backgrounds. By taking the helm in this way, your colleagues will see that they have an ally, and they will be encouraged to share their unique heritage and traditions.

Incorporating these practices into your leadership will engender a sense of belonging and interconnectedness among your team members. Everyone will feel that their contributions are valued, regardless of their background.

This will lead to more candid conversations, more harmonious exchanges, and, overall, a more productive environment.

Resilient Leader Profile: Bozoma Saint John

Bozoma Saint John is an exceptional American businessperson, marketing guru, and author who embodies resilience and cultural celebration. Her remarkable journey and accomplishments serve as an inspiration to leaders across all industries.

Bozoma Saint John's unwavering commitment to celebrating her culture sets her apart as a resilient leader. She embraces her heritage with pride and infuses it into her work, bringing a unique perspective that fosters understanding and appreciation. By openly celebrating her culture through her communication style as well as her hair and clothing, Bozoma Saint John paves the way for others to embrace their identities and diverse backgrounds in the workplace.

Bozoma Saint John has consistently championed diversity and inclusion through her leadership roles in prominent companies while also achieving record-breaking success that has been celebrated through numerous awards. She understands the importance of creating an inclusive environment where individuals from all walks of life feel valued and empowered, which has been a theme through many of her ad campaigns. Bozoma Saint John's efforts to elevate and amplify underrepresented voices have been instrumental in reshaping the business landscape.

As an author, Bozoma Saint John's work resonates deeply with individuals seeking to navigate the complexities of the corporate world while staying true to their cultural heritage and overcoming personal hurdles. Her writings encourage leaders to embrace their uniqueness and to be vulnerable, especially in life-altering moments, whether birth or death. Bozoma Saint John's insights and experiences serve as a guide for resilient leaders, showcasing the power of cultural celebration in driving success and creating positive change.

Bozoma Saint John's example inspires resilient leaders to integrate their cultural identities into their leadership styles, creating a workplace that thrives on diversity and innovation.

Lead by Example

Resilient leaders who belong to underrepresented groups have experienced the truth of working twice as hard to gain recognition. However, we aim to shift this paradigm and forge a more robust path for future leaders. We aim to model inclusive behavior and cultivate an environment where everyone feels respected and valued, especially younger leaders from underrepresented backgrounds. We must lead by example by addressing any instances of bias or discrimination that we encounter and taking immediate steps to rectify them.

In leadership strategy meetings, we should actively advocate for diversity in hiring and promotion opportunities, particularly for individuals from underrepresented communities. By mentoring and sponsoring others, we can assist them in overcoming barriers and advancing in their careers. As resilient leaders, we are responsible for leveraging our positions of influence to bring about positive change within our industry. Engaging in conferences, panel discussions, and public speaking engagements enables us to share our experiences, inspire others, and contribute to a more inclusive and diverse professional landscape.

Through these actions, we can establish a new standard for leadership that acknowledges the challenges faced by underrepresented groups and actively works towards dismantling systemic barriers. By fostering inclusivity, advocating for diversity, and using our influence to effect change, we can create a brighter future for the next generation of leaders, ensuring their voices are heard and their talents are recognized.

Chapter 4

EMPOWERING OTHERS: FIRST UNLEASHING THE POTENTIAL WITHIN

Dear Resilient Leader,

I hope this email finds you thriving in your leadership journey. As your guide on this journey, I wanted to share a valuable resource that can empower you as you inspire others.

I highly recommend the book You Owe You *by Eric Thomas in your pursuit of unleashing your potential. This insightful book is a powerful tool for resilient leaders like yourself, reminding us of the importance of taking ownership of our personal growth and development. As Eric Thomas aptly puts it, "What got you here won't get you there." This quote serves as a powerful reminder to continuously sharpen our leadership skills, evolving and adapting as we lead others.*

Empowering others begins with empowering ourselves. By investing in our own personal growth and leadership journey, we can effectively inspire and uplift those around us. "You Owe You" offers practical strategies and thought-provoking insights to help you tap into your full potential as a resilient leader.

As you navigate challenges and seize opportunities, I encourage you to continue sharpening your personal leadership skills. The Resilient Leader Program is dedicated to providing resources, support, and a community of like-minded leaders on this journey. Together, we can create a positive impact and empower those around us.

Thank you for your unwavering dedication to excellence in leadership. I believe in your ability to become a powerful change agent and inspire others to reach their full potential. If there's anything I can do to support you on your leadership journey, please reach out.

I wish you continued success and growth as a resilient leader.

Warm regards,

Jacqueline V. Twillie
President, ZeroGap.co
Creator, Resilient Leader Program

Empowerment in Leadership: Trusting Oneself to Make a Difference

Being a resilient leader means trusting yourself and having the confidence to make a positive impact. Empowerment in leadership is crucial for driving change and achieving success.

Here are four steps to help you embrace empowerment and trust your abilities:

First, get in the habit of trusting your intuition. Trusting your gut allows you to tap into your inner wisdom and make decisions based on your instincts. While data and analysis are essential, there are times when your gut feeling can guide you in the right direction. Cultivate self-trust and listen to your intuition when faced with difficult choices. Remember that your experiences and expertise have brought you where you are today.

Remembering that you have earned your leadership position for a reason is essential. You possess the skills, knowledge, and qualities necessary to lead effectively. Embrace your accomplishments, talents, and expertise. Recognize the value you bring to your team and organization. Remind yourself of past successes and the positive impact you have made. This self-affirmation will boost your confidence and empower you to take action with conviction.

Empowerment in leadership involves taking calculated risks. However, evaluating the potential risks and rewards is important before making decisions. Assess the potential outcomes, considering both short-term and long-term effects. Analyze the risks involved, and develop contingency plans to mitigate potential challenges. While taking risks is necessary for growth and progress, a thoughtful evaluation will enable you to make informed decisions that align with your goals and values.

Empowerment doesn't mean going it alone. Resilient leaders understand the value of seeking support and collaborating with others. Surround yourself with a network of trusted colleagues, mentors, or coaches who can offer guidance and different perspectives. Collaborate with your team members, leveraging their expertise and diverse insights. Empowerment is enhanced through collective effort and a supportive community.

By trusting your gut, acknowledging your worth, evaluating risks and rewards, and seeking support, you can embrace empowerment in leadership. These action steps will enable you to make confident decisions, take calculated risks, and ultimately make a positive difference as a resilient and empowered leader.

Developing Leadership in Others: Opportunities for Growth and Achievement

Leadership development is a powerful tool for empowering individuals within a community, extending beyond cultivating individual leaders. When people are equipped with leadership skills and given opportunities, they become catalysts for communal growth and achievement. Resilient leaders play a vital role in creating an environment that nurtures potential, encourages collaboration, and enhances collective success. This section explores the intersection of developing leadership in others as a form of empowerment, highlighting the communal opportunities for growth and achievement that arise from cultivating resilient leaders.

Empowerment Through Leadership Development

Developing leadership in others opens doors for individuals with untapped potential. It gives them the necessary tools, knowledge, and confidence to step up and make a difference. By investing in leadership development, communities create opportunities for people to discover and unleash their capabilities, fostering personal and professional growth.

Leadership development instills self-assurance in individuals, empowering them to take charge of their lives and make meaningful contributions. As people acquire leadership skills, they gain the confidence to tackle challenges, make decisions, and inspire others. This newfound confidence spreads throughout the community, creating a positive ripple effect.

Leadership development emphasizes effective communication, active listening, and collaboration. When individuals possess these skills, they can effectively articulate their ideas, build strong relationships, and bridge gaps within the community. This promotes understanding, unity, and cooperation, fostering a sense of belonging and shared purpose.

Developing leadership in others instills a sense of responsibility and accountability. Resilient leaders understand the importance of owning their actions and decisions, leading by example, and holding others accountable. This culture of accountability leads to increased productivity, innovation, and integrity within the community.

Communal Opportunities for Growth and Achievement

When leadership development is embraced at a communal level, it promotes shared leadership. This approach recognizes that leadership is not confined to a single individual but can be distributed among many. By encouraging diverse perspectives and engaging multiple leaders, communities tap into a wealth of ideas, experiences, and talents, leading to innovative solutions and sustainable growth.

Resilient leaders who have benefited from effective mentorship and coaching programs can pay it forward. By serving as mentors, they can guide and inspire emerging leaders, sharing their knowledge and experiences. This mentorship cycle creates a supportive ecosystem where ongoing leadership development strengthens the community's leadership pipeline.

Developing leadership in others fosters a collaborative mindset that drives collective projects and initiatives. Resilient leaders recognize the power of teamwork and actively seek opportunities to collaborate on community-based projects. These collaborations create spaces for diverse talents to unite, share resources, and tackle complex challenges, leading to transformative outcomes that benefit the entire community.

Empowered leaders are more likely to engage in community service and social impact initiatives. They utilize their skills and influence to address social issues, drive positive change, and uplift marginalized voices. Leadership development programs emphasizing social responsibility and community engagement create a cadre of leaders committed to serving the greater good.

Developing leadership in others as a form of empowerment goes beyond personal growth; it generates communal opportunities for growth and achievement. Resilient leaders who emerge from such programs bring about positive change by fostering collaboration, nurturing talent, and driving innovation. By investing in leadership development, communities can create a thriving ecosystem where individuals are empowered to reach their full potential and work together toward a brighter future.

Resilient Leader Profile: Valeisha Butterfield-Jones

Valeisha Butterfield-Jones is an exemplary leader known for her resilience, advocacy, and transformative impact on various industries. With her remarkable skills, strategic vision, and unwavering determination, she has consistently overcome challenges and emerged as a beacon of inspiration for aspiring leaders worldwide.

As a resilient leader, Valeisha Butterfield-Jones has consistently displayed the ability to navigate adversity and thrive in dynamic environments. She possesses a steadfast commitment to her goals, refusing to be deterred by setbacks. Her unwavering perseverance has been instrumental in overcoming obstacles and achieving remarkable success in her professional journey.

Valeisha Butterfield-Jones is a passionate advocate for diversity, inclusion, and equity. Through her leadership roles in the corporate world, she has consistently championed initiatives that promote equal opportunities and foster inclusive work cultures. She recognizes the importance of representation and has been a vocal advocate for marginalized communities, striving to create spaces where everyone feels valued and empowered.

Her ability to drive change is truly commendable. Valeisha Butterfield-Jones has been instrumental in spearheading innovative initiatives that have profoundly impacted society. Whether it is leveraging technology to bridge the digital divide, implementing programs to empower underserved communities, or leading campaigns for social justice, she consistently demonstrates a profound understanding of complex challenges and a unique ability to drive sustainable change.

Valeisha Butterfield-Jones possesses exceptional leadership skills that inspire those around her. Her collaborative approach, combined with her visionary mindset, allows her to build diverse and high-performing teams. She fosters an environment of trust and encourages open dialogue, empowering individuals to contribute their unique perspectives and ideas. Her leadership style not only cultivates innovation but also promotes personal growth and development among her team members.

In addition to her professional achievements, Valeisha Butterfield-Jones is known for her unwavering commitment to philanthropy and community engagement. She actively participates in various social initiatives, dedicating her time, resources, and influence to uplift others. Her passion for giving back and making a positive impact on society is a testament to her character as a resilient leader.

Valeisha Butterfield-Jones's accomplishments and impact have earned her numerous accolades and recognition throughout her career. However, she remains grounded, continuing to strive for excellence and inspire others to unlock their full potential.

Valeisha Butterfield-Jones is a resilient leader who exemplifies the qualities of determination, advocacy, and transformative leadership. Through her resilience, commitment to diversity and inclusion, ability to drive change, exceptional leadership skills, and dedication to philanthropy, she has become an inspiration for individuals seeking to make a lasting impact on their communities and the world.

Unapologetic Self-Advocacy: Empowering Yourself and Others to Succeed

Being Unapologetic and Code-Switching

The relationship between code-switching and being unapologetic is characterized by the delicate balance between conforming to societal expectations and embracing one's authentic self. Code-switching involves adapting language, behavior, or cultural expressions to fit into specific social or professional contexts. While it can be a strategic tool for navigating different environments and gaining acceptance, it may also entail suppressing or altering aspects of one's identity.

On the other hand, being unapologetic entails embracing and expressing one's true self without fear or hesitation, regardless of societal norms or expectations. It involves prioritizing authenticity and refusing to conform or apologize for one's identity.

Resilient leaders can take several steps to remain true to themselves in the context of code-switching. Firstly, self-awareness plays a crucial role as they understand their values, strengths, and identity. This deep self-awareness enables them to recognize moments when they might compromise their authenticity through code-switching.

Furthermore, prioritizing authenticity becomes a guiding principle for resilient leaders. They consciously align their actions and decisions with their true selves, even in challenging or unfamiliar environments. By making deliberate choices to stay true to their values and beliefs, they establish a solid foundation for their leadership. They also embrace their unique perspectives and experiences, understanding the value they bring. Recognizing their diverse background's significance, they contribute distinct insights and ideas that enrich their leadership approach.

By combining self-awareness, authenticity, and empowerment, resilient leaders reconcile the complexities of code-switching and being unapologetic. They establish a firm grounding in their identity and values, enabling them to lead with integrity and inspire others to do the same.

Resilient Leader Profile: Eric Thomas, The Hip Hop Preacher

Eric Thomas, also known as the Hip Hop Preacher, is an acclaimed motivational speaker, author, and educator who has inspired millions worldwide. Through his powerful speeches, energetic delivery, and relatable storytelling, Thomas symbolizes resilience and transformation. This profile explores the life and achievements of Eric Thomas, highlighting his journey as a resilient leader and the impact he has made on individuals and communities.

Born and raised in Detroit, Michigan, Eric Thomas experienced a challenging childhood. He grew up in a single-parent household, faced homelessness, and struggled academically. Despite these adversities, Thomas was unwaveringly determined to change his circumstances and make a positive impact.

Eric Thomas's pivotal moment came when he encountered a mentor who encouraged him to pursue education. He earned his GED and obtained a bachelor's degree, a master's degree, and a Ph.D. in education. Thomas's transformation fueled his desire to inspire others to reach their full potential, regardless of their background or circumstances.

With a unique blend of motivational speaking and the influence of hip-hop culture, Eric Thomas developed his signature style as the Hip Hop Preacher. He began delivering powerful speeches that combined personal anecdotes, motivational messages, and the energetic spirit of hip-hop. Thomas's delivery resonated with audiences, especially young people, captivated by his authenticity and relatability.

As a resilient leader, Eric Thomas has touched the lives of millions through his speeches, books, and online presence. His messages of perseverance, self-belief, and personal responsibility have inspired individuals from diverse backgrounds, encouraging them to overcome obstacles and achieve their goals. Thomas has become a sought-after speaker, addressing audiences worldwide at schools, colleges, corporations, and conferences.

Eric Thomas has authored several books, including *The Secret to Success*, *Average Skill Phenomenal Will*, and *Greatness Is Upon You*. These books provide practical insights and strategies for personal growth, emphasizing the importance of resilience, discipline, and embracing one's unique journey. Thomas's work extends beyond motivational speaking, as he is also an educator and a professor at Michigan State University.

Driven by his desire to give back and positively impact, Eric Thomas is actively involved in philanthropic efforts. He has partnered with various organizations and initiatives to empower young people, promote education, and support underserved communities. Thomas's commitment to community engagement further exemplifies his role as a resilient leader who inspires and actively contributes to societal change.

Eric Thomas, the Hip Hop Preacher, is a shining example of a resilient leader who has overcome adversity and dedicated his life to inspiring others. Through his powerful speeches, books, and philanthropy, Thomas has transformed countless lives, motivating individuals to believe in themselves, embrace their unique journeys, and pursue excellence. As a symbol of resilience and transformation, Eric Thomas remains a beacon of hope and empowerment, leaving an indelible mark on those who encounter his message.

Chapter 5

CULTIVATING SELF-AWARENESS: THE KEY TO AUTHENTIC LEADERSHIP

Dear Resilient Leaders,

In the pursuit of effective leadership, one aspect stands out as essential: self-awareness. Understanding ourselves, our emotions, and our impact on others is a cornerstone of authentic leadership. Today, I want to emphasize the power of self-awareness and how it can positively influence our leadership style and relationships.

Self-awareness is the foundation upon which we build our leadership journey. It involves recognizing our strengths, weaknesses, values, beliefs, and emotions. By developing a deep understanding of ourselves, we gain insight into our actions, decisions, and interactions with others.

One vital aspect of self-awareness is understanding our impact on others. As leaders, our words, actions, and demeanor significantly influence those we lead. By being aware of how our behavior affects others, we can tailor our approach to inspire, motivate, and empower our team members.

Here are a few vital benefits of cultivating self-awareness as leaders:

Building Trust: *When self-aware, we can align our intentions and actions, fostering trust among our team members. By understanding how our behavior is perceived, we can ensure that our efforts are consistent with our values, building credibility and confidence in the process.*

Emotional Intelligence: *Self-awareness is closely linked to emotional intelligence. By recognizing our own emotions and understanding how they influence our behavior, we can better manage our reactions and empathize with the feelings of others. This enables us to create a supportive and inclusive work environment.*

Authenticity: *Authentic leadership stems from self-awareness. When we deeply understand who we are, we can lead authentically, embracing our unique strengths and values. This genuine approach attracts and inspires others, fostering a culture of openness and collaboration.*

Continuous Growth: *Self-awareness allows us to identify personal and professional growth areas. By acknowledging our weaknesses, we can seek development opportunities through training, mentorship, or self-reflection. This commitment to growth benefits us as individuals and sets an example for our team members.*

As resilient leaders, you have already demonstrated the ability to adapt and persevere through challenging times. By cultivating self-awareness, you can enhance your leadership skills and positively impact your team and organization. Please take time for self-reflection. Engage in practices like journaling or mindfulness and seek feedback from trusted colleagues or mentors. Continuously developing self-awareness will strengthen your ability to lead authentically and create a positive and empowering work environment.

Remember, self-awareness is an ongoing journey. It requires self-reflection, openness to feedback, and a genuine commitment to personal growth. As you embrace the power of self-awareness, you will unlock new levels of leadership effectiveness and positively influence those around you.

I wish that every day, you uncover new dimensions of yourself and that every discovery propels you forward in your leadership endeavors.

With warm regards,

Jacqueline V. Twillie
Founder of ZeroGap.co
Creator of the Resilient Leaders Program

THE POWER OF SELF-AWARENESS: UNDERSTANDING YOUR IMPACT ON OTHERS

If you are invested in building a space where healthy relationships are the norm, you must understand your emotions, triggers, and biases. By the way, it is worth noting that we all have biases. I want to emphasize this very important point: We all have biases. Biases are a part of us as long as we breathe. An article in the *Harvard Business Review* entitled "Are You Aware of Your Biases?" highlights the importance of recognizing and addressing our biases. Its author, Carmen Acton, emphasizes how easy it can be to identify biases in others without acknowledging our own subconscious biases. Her article suggests that acknowledging these biases and educating ourselves can help improve our leadership skills, particularly for new managers.

The first step in addressing biases is to be aware of them and question whether we hold stereotypes or assumptions about certain social groups. As managers, it is crucial to acknowledge and leverage the differences within our teams. By identifying our unconscious assumptions, we can begin to unlearn them.

When someone points out our unconscious biases, it is important not to become defensive. Instead, we should assume positive intent and view their feedback as an opportunity to learn and grow. Seeking feedback from a diverse group of peers can provide valuable insights into how we are perceived and help us stay accountable as we strive to change our behaviors.

The article also encourages embracing diverse perspectives by expanding our networks. If our close circle of colleagues resembles us, actively seeking out connections with individuals from different backgrounds is essential. Joining employee resource groups or engaging with colleagues who have diverse experiences can contribute to a broader perspective and understanding of different viewpoints.

Overall, Acton emphasizes the need for self-awareness and continuous learning in order to overcome biases and create inclusive environments. By acknowledging our own biases and actively working to unlearn them, we can become more effective leaders and foster diversity and inclusion within our teams.

Self-awareness is a crucial trait for resilient leaders, and there are several tools that can help cultivate it. The first tool is to identify and understand your emotions, recognizing how they can impact your interactions with others. By being aware of your emotional state, you can respond thoughtfully rather than impulsively, fostering a positive and conducive environment for connection.

Another tool is to explore your triggers, whether they are certain situations, behaviors, or individuals. By recognizing these triggers, you can proactively manage your responses and prevent unintended conflicts or breakdowns in communication. It's important to be honest with yourself about your biases and work towards overcoming them. Challenging your assumptions and seeking diverse perspectives can help foster a more inclusive and open-minded approach to building connections.

Regulating your responses and behaviors is another key tool of self-awareness. This involves pausing before reacting, considering the impact of your words and actions, and choosing constructive communication methods. By practicing self-regulation, you create a safe space for others to express themselves and encourage open dialogue.

Additionally, it is valuable to seek feedback from others regarding your communication style, approach, and impact. Listening to their perspectives and considering how you can improve your self-awareness and connection-building skills can lead to growth as a leader. Committing to lifelong learning and personal growth through activities like mindfulness exercises, journaling, or professional development opportunities can enhance self-awareness and promote healthy connections with team members.

Ultimately, self-awareness is an ongoing journey that requires dedication and a commitment to personal growth. By prioritizing self-awareness, resilient leaders can regulate their responses, manage biases, and create an environment that fosters healthy connections. Building stronger connections with team members and establishing a positive and supportive work environment are the rewards of continuously developing this skill.

Personal accountability plays a vital role in the daily actions of resilient leaders to avoid falling into the trap of proving themselves to those who view them as stereotypes. Here's how personal accountability can help:

Resilient leaders who practice personal accountability prioritize being authentic and genuine to themselves. They understand they don't need to prove themselves based on others' stereotypes or expectations. Instead, they focus on staying true to their values, strengths, and unique perspectives.

Personal accountability involves regularly reflecting on one's thoughts, behaviors, and actions. Resilient leaders use this self-reflection to recognize any tendencies to fall into the trap of proving themselves or conforming to stereotypes. They take responsibility for their actions and actively work to overcome these tendencies.

Resilient, personally accountable leaders set clear goals that align with their core values and aspirations. They ensure that their daily actions and decisions align with these goals rather than being driven by the need to prove themselves to others. By staying focused on their objectives, they can maintain their authenticity and avoid getting caught up in proving themselves.

Personal accountability helps resilient leaders build confidence and self-assurance. When they take ownership of their actions and beliefs, they become less reliant on external validation or approval. They trust their abilities and value their unique contributions, enabling them to effectively navigate stereotypes' challenges.

Resilient leaders practicing personal accountability understand that setbacks and obstacles may come their way due to stereotypes. However, they view these challenges as opportunities for growth and learning rather than as a validation of the stereotypes. They bounce back, learn from setbacks, and persist with determination and resilience.

Personal accountability involves seeking support from a trusted network of mentors, peers, or allies. Resilient leaders surround themselves with individuals who believe in their potential and support their growth. This support network can provide guidance and encouragement and help them stay accountable to their core values, reducing the impact of external stereotypes.

Personal accountability empowers resilient leaders to stay true to themselves, align their actions with their values and goals, maintain confidence, and overcome the traps of proving themselves to those who view them as stereotypes. By practicing personal accountability, they can navigate the male-dominated space with resilience and authenticity.

REFLECTIVE LEADERSHIP: EVALUATING BEHAVIORS AND ACTIONS

AHA Method

The AHA process encompasses three core elements: attitude, habits, and actions. Attitude refers to your perspective and outlook on a given situation. Adopting a positive mindset, addressing limiting beliefs, and cultivating gratitude can set the foundation for success. Habits, the second element, are the behaviors you repeatedly engage in. Identifying habits that support your goals, focusing on one or two at a time, and creating a plan for their establishment are key steps in this process. Finally, actions are the steps you take to achieve your goals. Breaking down your goals into manageable steps, creating an action plan, and consistently taking action, no matter how small, are essential in moving closer to success. By integrating attitude, habits, and actions, the AHA process empowers you to realize your potential and attain a sense of fulfillment.

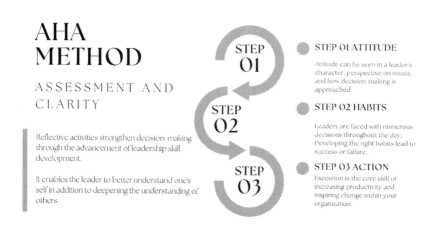

Diagram: AHA with three core elements: attitude, habits, and actions.

A - ATTITUDE

The first core element of the AHA process is attitude. Your attitude is your outlook or perspective on a given situation. It can be positive or negative and impact how you approach and tackle challenges. To cultivate the right attitude, you should:

Start with a positive mindset - believe that you can achieve your goals and that you can overcome any obstacles. Identify and address any limiting beliefs that might be holding you back. Cultivate gratitude and focus on what you have rather than what you lack.

H - HABITS

As resilient leaders, harnessing the power of habits is a vital tool in the AHA process. Habits, the behaviors we engage in unconsciously, hold significant sway over our success and well-being. To cultivate positive habits, we can utilize the following steps:

1. Recognize and evaluate the habits that impact our progress toward our goals. Identifying the habits that contribute positively or hinder our advancement is crucial for effective self-awareness and improvement.

2. Select one or two pivotal habits to focus on at any given time. By narrowing our focus, we can direct our energy and efforts toward developing these key habits, ensuring a more manageable and effective approach.

3. Develop a comprehensive plan to establish the desired habit. This plan should include specific actions and details on when and how to implement them. We can create a roadmap to success and ensure consistent progress by mapping out the necessary steps.

By utilizing these tools, resilient leaders can harness the power of habits, enabling personal growth, enhancing effectiveness, and ultimately achieving long-term success and well-being.

A - ACTIONS

The AHA process's third and final core element is actions. Actions are the steps taken to achieve your goals. To ensure effective action, explore how to break down your goals into smaller, more manageable steps. By creating a detailed action plan outlining the steps required to reach your objectives, you provide a clear roadmap for success. Taking consistent action toward your goals is crucial, even if the measures are tiny. Consistency is a powerful tool for progressing and moving closer to the desired outcome.

Resilient leaders can adapt the AHA process into their weekly, monthly, quarterly, or annual reflection and self-awareness practices. Leaders can cultivate a resilient mindset and enhance effectiveness by incorporating attitudes, habits, and actions into their routines.

During regular reflections, leaders can assess their attitude by examining their perspectives on recent challenges and achievements. They can identify any negative or limiting beliefs hindering their progress and consciously work on shifting them to a growth mindset. Expressing gratitude for accomplishments and focusing on lessons learned rather than dwelling on setbacks can also contribute to a positive attitude.

Regarding habits, leaders can review their ongoing behaviors and evaluate their alignment with their goals. They can identify habits that have been supportive and reinforce them further. Additionally, leaders can select one or two essential habits to focus on improving or establishing, creating a plan that outlines specific actions and timelines for implementation. Regular check-ins can help leaders track their progress and make necessary adjustments.

Lastly, leaders should take consistent actions toward their goals. They can break down their objectives into manageable steps and create an action plan outlining the necessary actions to achieve them. By scheduling and prioritizing these actions, leaders can ensure progress is made regularly. Even small steps taken consistently can contribute to long-term success.

Resilient leaders can continually assess and improve their attitudes, habits, and actions by integrating the AHA process into their reflection and self-awareness routines. This systematic approach enables leaders to adapt and grow, leading to increased effectiveness and greater fulfillment in their personal and professional lives.

The book *The Gap and the Gain* by Dan Sullivan introduces a powerful concept that complements the AHA method. The central idea is that unsuccessful people focus on "The Gap," while successful individuals focus on "The Gain."

The Gap refers to the tendency to measure oneself against an ideal or a future state that is often unattainable or constantly moving. This mindset can lead to unhappiness and dissatisfaction because the perfect is always out of reach. Many highly ambitious people fall into this trap, continually comparing themselves to an unachievable standard.

In contrast, The Gain involves measuring one's progress against their previous self. By focusing on how far they have come and their progress, individuals can experience a sense of happiness, confidence, and satisfaction. This positive mindset encourages further growth and motivates individuals to pursue new goals, leading to increasing success.

The Gap and the Gain aligns well with the AHA method's emphasis on attitude, habits, and actions. Adopting a positive attitude and mindset, as advocated in the AHA method, involves cultivating gratitude and acknowledging progress. By measuring progress against oneself and recognizing the gains achieved, individuals can build a strong foundation for success.

Furthermore, integrating *The Gap and the Gain* into the AHA method can help individuals in their habit formation process. Instead of solely focusing on the ideal habits they aspire to develop, they can appreciate and acknowledge their already established habits. This recognition of progress can boost motivation and provide the confidence to create new patterns.

Ultimately, combining the AHA method and the principles presented in *The Gap and the Gain* offers individuals a comprehensive approach to personal growth and success. By emphasizing a positive attitude, recognizing progress, and consistently taking action, individuals can harness their potential, experience fulfillment, and achieve their goals.

LEADING WITH PURPOSE: ALIGNING ACTIONS WITH VALUES

Dear Resilient Leaders,

As always, this email comes with my hopes for your mental, spiritual, and physical well-being. In my previous message to you, I shared some thoughts on the benefits of self-awareness in your relationships with others. Today, I want to emphasize self-awareness as it relates to our personal value system.

Self-awareness goes beyond mere introspection.

I founded ZeroGap and the Resilient Leaders Program, because I believe that catalyzing change in the professional sphere is vital for building a better and fairer society. Throughout my career, I have witnessed the transformative power of self-awareness in leaders who are determined to make a lasting impact. It is my passion to help individuals like you enhance their self-awareness and unlock their full leadership potential.

I am writing to you, because I have a feeling that you and I share a common sense of purpose to effect change and help diversity thrive wherever we are. Today, let me highlight introspection and self-discovery as part of this mission. Take the time to reflect on your leadership values—the principles and beliefs that drive your decisions and actions. Consider the values that define you as a leader and resonate with your authentic self. This exercise will provide you with a solid foundation upon which you can navigate the complexities of leadership with integrity and resilience.

If you're interested in deepening your self-awareness and exploring your personal leadership values further, I encourage you to explore the Resilient Leaders Program, a transformative initiative designed to empower leaders like you. The program offers a supportive environment for growth and self-discovery through interactive workshops, coaching sessions, and resources.

Remember: Your own experiences are your doorway to others and to the rest of the world. You begin inspiring change all around you when you first look within. If your experiences and values are the door, then introspection is the key to unlocking your potential to shape this world for the better.

Thank you for your time and dedication to personal and professional growth. Let's continue embodying resilience, authenticity, and transformative leadership.

Warm regards,

Jacqueline V. Twillie
President of ZeroGap.co
Founder of the Resilient Leaders Program

Resilient Leader Strategy for Enhancing Value Awareness

In the face of countless challenges that require unwavering dedication and adaptability, leaders find themselves navigating through turbulent times. In order to effectively steer through these tumultuous waters, it becomes imperative for leaders to establish a robust groundwork rooted in their personal and professional values. By clearly defining and wholeheartedly embracing these values, resilient leaders can stay true to their authentic sense of purpose and also pave a path toward triumph. This section aims to provide leaders with a comprehensive step-by-step guide, facilitating the seamless integration of their values into their personal and professional spheres.

Step 1: *Define the terms "personal values" and "professional values"*

Personal values are the fundamental beliefs and principles that shape an individual's character and drive their choices, actions, and decision-making processes. A personal value system often encompasses traits such as honesty, loyalty, respect, and freedom. In contrast, professional values refer to the principles and beliefs that guide behavior and decision-making within a work or career context. They may include integrity, teamwork, excellence, customer service, and other values relevant to professional settings.

Step 2: Brainstorm a list of values

Take the time to reflect on the values that hold significance to you. Engage in introspection and compile a list of values that resonate with your core being. This list can include values such as honesty, trust, creativity, efficiency, respect, empathy, professionalism, fairness, and responsibility. If needed, online resources can provide comprehensive lists of values to choose from, expanding your options and helping you identify values you may not have considered before.

Step 3: Prioritize your values

Once you have compiled a list of values, it's crucial to prioritize them according to their importance in your life. Delve deeper into your introspection and consider questions like "Which values do I believe in the most?" or "Which values do I want to guide my actions and decisions?" By answering these questions, you can establish a hierarchy of values that aligns with your personal and professional aspirations.

Step 4: Identify how your values show up in your life

Reflect on how your prioritized values manifest in your day-to-day existence. Explore how these values influence your relationships, hobbies, and involvement in the community. Additionally, contemplate significant life choices and decisions you have made and how your values may have played a role in shaping those moments. Understanding the impact of your values on various aspects of your life will provide clarity and help you strengthen your alignment with them.

Step 5: Consider your workplace values

Take a moment to examine the values that hold significance in your workplace. Consider the values promoted by your organization or industry, as well as those valued by your colleagues or clients. Reflect on how closely these workplace values align with your own. Evaluating this alignment can shed light on the congruence between your personal and professional values and help you determine the level of harmony within your work environment.

Step 6: Assess your actions

Evaluate whether your actions consistently align with your values. Examine past instances where you may have acted in a way that conflicted with your values, as well as occasions when you felt proud of your behavior because it aligned with your values. By identifying these experiences, you can gain insight into the areas where your actions may need adjustment and use them as guideposts for future decision-making.

Step 7: Continuously evaluate and refine your values

Recognize that personal growth and change are constant elements of life. As you evolve, your values may also undergo transformation. Regularly assess and refine your values to ensure they remain in alignment with who you are and who you aspire to become. This ongoing process may involve adding new values to your list or reordering your existing priorities to reflect your changing perspectives and experiences.

By following these steps, resilient leaders can gain a deep understanding of their personal and professional values. This knowledge serves as a compass, providing direction and purpose in the face of adversity. By embracing their values and aligning their actions with them, leaders can foster an environment of authenticity and integrity, inspiring those around them and cultivating resilience within their teams.

Dear Resilient Leaders,

As leaders in male-dominated industries, you face unique challenges and obstacles. You may constantly have to prove yourself, battle stereotypes, and navigate complex power dynamics. In such an environment, it can be challenging to maintain a sense of purpose and stay true to your values.

Based on my firsthand experiences with these challenges, I want to emphasize how important clarity is in the impact you seek. Knowing your values and beliefs and how they align with your goals can help you stay focused and motivated in adversity. It will also help you make difficult decisions when faced with ethical dilemmas.

Having clarity on the impact you seek to have will also enable you to be intentional in your actions and choices. You can choose to be a trailblazer and pave the way for others, or you can choose to conform to the dominant culture. Whatever you decide, clearly understanding your goals and values will help you stay true to yourself and your purpose.

In addition to clarity, it is essential to surround yourself with a supportive network. Seek mentors and sponsors who can guide you and provide valuable insights and feedback. Build relationships with colleagues who share your values and can offer support and encouragement.

Remember, resilience is not just about bouncing back from challenges. It is also about the courage to stand up for what you believe in and remain true to your values. Having clarity on the impact you seek to have will enable you to do just that.

With your resilience, determination, and clarity of purpose, you can overcome any challenge and achieve the impact you seek.

Sincerely,

Jacqueline V. Twillie
Founder of ZeroGap.co
Creator of the Resilient Leaders Program

The Importance of Clarity in Values

Clarity of values plays a vital role in helping resilient leaders navigate male-dominated industries. A clear understanding of one's values and beliefs helps individuals stay focused on their goals and maintain their integrity in facing challenges and obstacles.

In male-dominated industries, underrepresented leaders may face pressure to conform to the dominant culture and compromise their values to fit in. This can lead to feelings of discomfort and dissonance, making it challenging to maintain a positive outlook and remain resilient during periods of change and stress.

Having clarity of values helps individuals stay true to themselves and their beliefs, even in challenging situations. It provides a sense of purpose and direction, helping individuals stay focused on their goals and maintain their integrity. This, in turn, can help individuals feel more empowered and resilient, even when facing adversity.

In addition, having clarity of values can also help individuals make better decisions and communicate more effectively with others. It provides a common ground for understanding and can help individuals build relationships based on shared values and beliefs. Consider these steps to guide you in achieving this clarity.

Step 1: Reflect on your beliefs and values

Take some time to reflect on what matters most to you. Think about your core beliefs and values and what drives you. Consider what brings you the most satisfaction and fulfillment in life. Write down your thoughts and observations in a journal or notebook.

Step 2: Identify your strengths and weaknesses

Understanding your strengths and weaknesses can help you clarify what matters most. Assess your skills and capabilities, and think about what you enjoy doing most. Identify areas where you need improvement and focus on developing those areas.

Step 3: Define your purpose

Define your purpose and identify what motivates you. Consider what you want to accomplish and what legacy you want to leave behind. Think about how you can use your talents and skills to impact the world positively.

Step 4: Assess your current situation

Take a step back and assess your current situation. Think about the people, situations, and circumstances that are most important to you. Identify areas of your life that may be out of balance or in conflict with your values.

Step 5: Align your actions with your values

Review your goals and actions, and determine whether they align with your values. Make adjustments to ensure your efforts are consistent with your beliefs and values.

Step 6: Seek feedback and support

Seek feedback and support from others to gain a different perspective on your values and beliefs. Connect with people who share your values and can offer guidance and support as you align your actions with your values.

Step 7: Continuously evaluate and adjust

Regularly evaluate and adjust your values and actions as you grow and evolve. Remain open to new perspectives and experiences that may challenge your beliefs and values. Continuously align your actions with your values to maintain a sense of purpose and fulfillment.

By following these steps, you stay focused on what matters most to you. With a clear sense of purpose and direction, you can navigate the challenges of male-dominated industries with greater confidence and resilience. Here is a list of 50 values to help get you started on defining your core beliefs:

Resilient Leadership Value	Definition
Authenticity	Being genuine and true to oneself
Compassion	Showing empathy and care for others
Courage	The ability to face difficult or challenging situations
Creativity	The use of imagination to produce original ideas
Dependability	Being reliable and trustworthy
Determination	Firmness of purpose and a strong resolve
Excellence	The quality of being outstanding or exceptionally good
Fairness	Treating others in a just and unbiased manner
Faith	Trust or belief in something or someone
Flexibility	The ability to adapt and change easily
Forgiveness	Granting pardon or letting go of resentment
Friendship	A close and supportive relationship between people
Gratitude	A feeling of appreciation or thankfulness
Growth	The process of developing or maturing
Happiness	A state of joy and contentment
Health	The overall well-being of the body and mind

Resilient Leadership Value	Definition
Honesty	Being truthful and having integrity
Humility	Modesty and a lack of arrogance
Independence	The ability to think and act freely
Innovation	The introduction of new ideas or methods
Integrity	The adherence to moral and ethical principles
Intelligence	The capacity for learning, reasoning, and understanding
Justice	Fairness and equity in treatment and behavior
Kindness	Being considerate and compassionate
Knowledge	Information, facts, and skills acquired through learning
Leadership	The ability to guide and inspire others
Learning	The acquisition of knowledge and skills
Loyalty	Faithfulness and devotion to a person or cause
Open-mindedness	Willingness to consider new ideas and perspectives
Optimism	A positive and hopeful outlook on life
Passion	Strong enthusiasm or intense desire
Patience	The ability to endure delay or difficulties
Perseverance	Persistence and continued effort
Persistence	Firm and continued determination
Personal development	The ongoing process of improving oneself
Power	The ability to influence or control

Resilient Leadership Value	Definition
Professionalism	Conducting oneself with competence and integrity
Purpose	A sense of meaning and direction in life
Quality	The standard of excellence or superiority
Respect	Showing esteem, honor, and consideration
Responsibility	Being accountable for one's actions and obligations
Service	Providing assistance or help to others
Spirituality	The search for and connection with a higher power
Strength	The capacity to withstand challenges and adversity
Success	Achievement of goals or desired outcomes
Teamwork	Collaborating and working together towards a common goal
Trust	Reliance on the integrity and reliability of others
Wisdom	Deep understanding and good judgment
Work ethic	The principles and values that guide one's work habits

Once you've chosen the core tenets that define your personal life, you can begin to apply them or adapt them to your professional value system. The following are a list of some ways you can practice and exercise your values in the workplace.

Building support networks: They surround themselves with individuals who appreciate and support their authentic selves. A strong support network helps them feel validated and encouraged to be unapologetic in their leadership style.

Challenging societal norms: Resilient leaders challenge societal norms and expectations by advocating for diversity, inclusion, and authenticity. They use their influence and platform to create spaces where people can be themselves without fear of judgment or reprisal.

Education and awareness: They continuously educate themselves about identity, diversity, and inclusion issues. This knowledge equips them with the tools to address biases and stereotypes within themselves and their organizations or communities.

By embodying these qualities and taking these actions, resilient leaders can navigate the delicate balance between code-switching and being unapologetic. They create environments where individuals can bring their whole selves to the table, fostering a culture of authenticity, inclusion, and growth.

Embracing an unapologetic mindset and maintaining a strong connection to core values can be further reinforced by adopting a growth mindset. While being unapologetic encourages individuals to stay true to themselves, a growth mindset emphasizes the importance of adaptability and continuous personal development. By embracing a growth mindset, individuals can navigate the complexities of life while staying grounded in their core values. This mindset enables them to see challenges as opportunities for growth, learn from setbacks, and adapt their approaches without compromising authenticity. It allows them to remain rooted in their values while embracing the inevitable changes and transformations that come their way, fostering a harmonious synergy between being unapologetic and adaptive to the dynamic nature of their personal and professional worlds.

Chapter 6

BOOSTING RESILIENCE: STRENGTHENING YOUR INNER CORE

Dear Resilient Leader,

I wanted to take a moment to delve into the topic of resilience and discuss three key elements for bolstering your inner core to overcome challenges and setbacks.

The fast-paced changes in our modern world can often be overwhelming, presenting us with unexpected hurdles and disruptions. However, by cultivating resilience, we can transform these challenges into opportunities for personal growth and development. Resilience empowers us to bounce back from setbacks, maintain focus amidst the chaos, and embrace change with an open mind.

On a basic level, resilience can be broken down into three parts: preparing for potential challenges, adjusting to changing circumstances, and exercising self-care to recover from the unforeseen. After practicing resilience in these ways, our efforts will culminate in growth. By integrating these three components into our lives, we can fortify our inner core and develop resilience that will serve us well in the face of adversity. Remember, resilience is not merely about bouncing back; it is about learning, growing, and thriving in the face of challenges.

By continuing to focus on building resilience, both within yourself and your organization, you create an environment that inspires others to embrace change.

I encourage you to reflect on these components and consider how you can further enhance your own resilience while supporting and nurturing it within your team. Together, we can face the future with confidence and emerge stronger than ever.

I wish you continued resilience and success on your leadership journey.

Jacqueline V. Twillie
Founder of Zerogap.co
Creator of the Resilient Leaders Program

Resilience in a Changing World: Adapting and Thriving

Three Essential Components for Building Resiliency

Preparation: *The first step in building resilience is preparing ourselves for potential challenges and hardships. What does this look like in practice? First, this means identifying potential stressors. Stressors can include work-related issues, financial difficulties, or personal conflicts. After stressors are identified, we can anticipate potential obstacles based on what is causing us stress. Finally, we can develop proactive coping strategies based on our strengths, weaknesses, emotional intelligence, and opportunities for self-improvement.*

For example, if work-related stress is a potential stressor, we can develop coping strategies such as practicing mindfulness, taking breaks throughout the day, and delegating tasks when possible. If financial difficulties are a potential stressor, we can create a budget, save money, and seek financial advice. If personal conflicts are a potential stressor, we can practice effective communication skills, seek support from friends and family, or consider therapy. By preparing and developing coping strategies, we can better manage our stress levels, reduce the impact of potential stressors on our mental and physical health, and build resilience.

Adaptation: The next step is to adapt to changing circumstances. Adaptability lies at the core of resilience. It encompasses our ability to adjust and respond effectively to changing circumstances. By embracing a growth mindset and remaining open to new ideas and approaches, we enhance our capacity to navigate uncertainty. Embracing change rather than resisting it allows us to discover innovative solutions and seize opportunities that may arise from unexpected situations.

Being adaptable means being able to pivot and change course when necessary. It requires a willingness to take risks, embrace uncertainty, and try new things. It also involves learning from mistakes and failures instead of dwelling on them. Adapting to change is not always easy, but essential for personal and professional growth.

When we face challenging circumstances, seeking support from others can also be crucial in helping us adapt. Whether seeking guidance from a mentor, connecting with colleagues, or speaking with a therapist, reaching out for support is a sign of strength, not weakness.

Adapting to changing circumstances is essential for building resilience. It requires flexibility, openness to new ideas, a willingness to take risks, and seeking support when necessary. Adapting to change can be challenging, but it is a vital component of personal and professional growth. For example, suppose an individual has experienced a setback in their career. In that case, they may take the opportunity to reassess their goals and priorities and to identify areas where they need to improve their skills or knowledge. By doing so, they can develop a plan to address these areas and work towards achieving their goals. Similarly, if an individual has experienced success, they may reflect on what they did well and try replicating those behaviors in future situations.

Self-Care: Resilience is only sustainable through self-care. Taking care of our physical, mental, and emotional well-being is essential for maintaining a robust inner core. This includes practicing mindfulness, engaging in regular exercise, ensuring sufficient rest, and fostering healthy relationships. When we prioritize self-care, we replenish our energy reserves and equip ourselves to handle challenges with clarity and strength.

Growth: Depending on how you look at it, growth could be a fourth aspect of resilience or the result of it. Individuals should apply these lessons to future situations rather than dwell on past failures or successes. This process involves developing a positive outlook on life and a sense of purpose, which can help individuals stay motivated and optimistic during difficult times.

Ultimately, the growth step is crucial for building resilience because it helps individuals develop a sense of self-awareness and a growth mindset, which allows them to learn and adapt to new challenges continually. By reflecting on and learning from their experiences, individuals can become more confident in their abilities and better equipped to handle future setbacks.

Jacqueline V. Twillie

Self-Care and Well-being: Nurturing Your Resilience

Dear Resilient Leaders,

As much as I applaud you for the strength and tenacity it has taken you to reach this stage in your life, I never want you to forget that you are also worthy of rest. As important as it is to remain steadfast in the face of obstacles, it is also important to acknowledge your humanity—to leave space in your day for joy and time in your busy schedule to reset and recharge.

The past year has been incredibly challenging. Many have experienced burnout and exhaustion. We have been forced to adapt to new working methods, navigate uncertainty, and deal with personal and professional setbacks. In the face of all this, it can be easy to forget the importance of taking a break and finding moments of levity.

You have likely faced additional challenges related to being underrepresented in your industry. It is essential to acknowledge that these challenges are not your fault and that you are not alone in facing them. However, it is also important to recognize that resilience and determination are significant assets in navigating these challenges.

So, I encourage you to take a step back, reflect on your accomplishments, and find ways to find pleasure in your life. This might mean taking a vacation, spending time with loved ones, or pursuing a hobby that brings you happiness. It is okay to take a break and prioritize your well-being.

Always remember that being resilient does not mean you have to be invincible. It means having the strength to overcome challenges while also caring for yourself. By tending to your needs, you will be better equipped to navigate the challenges ahead and continue to thrive in your industry.

Thank you for all that you do, and please do not hesitate to reach out if there is anything I can do to support you.

Best regards,

Jacqueline V. Twillie
Founder of ZeroGap.co
Creator of the Resilient Leaders Program

Burnout and the Fallout

In recent years, leaders have moved away from a hustle-hard culture to one that's more focused on the right alignment and flow. With this shift, there's been more discussion in the workplace about the impact of stress on a leader's well-being. While resilience is a necessary skill, it shouldn't come at the cost of one's health. Symptoms of stress that lead to burnout associated with #teamnosleep are unacceptable in the modern workplace. Burnout is a complex issue influenced by various factors, including work-related stressors, organizational culture, and individual characteristics. While there isn't an abundance of specific research comparing the risk of burnout between underrepresented leaders and white men in leadership, we can discuss some general factors that may contribute to burnout among underrepresented leaders.

Discrimination and Bias: Underrepresented leaders often face discrimination and bias in the workplace, which can increase their risk of burnout. Experiences of prejudice, stereotyping, and microaggressions can lead to chronic stress and emotional exhaustion. A study by Purvanova and Muros (2010) found that workplace discrimination was positively related to burnout symptoms.

Lack of Representation: The pressure of being a minority in a leadership position can be overwhelming. Underrepresented leaders may face higher expectations, scrutiny, and the burden of being seen as a representative of their entire group. This added responsibility can contribute to burnout. A study by Offermann et al. (2014) suggests that the burden of representation can lead to increased emotional labor and psychological strain.

Limited Support Networks: Underrepresented leaders often need more access to supportive networks and mentors who can understand their unique challenges. This lack of support can exacerbate feelings of isolation and increase the risk of burnout. A study by Sekaquaptewa et al. (2017) found that the presence of same-gender and same-race mentors reduced the risk of burnout among underrepresented employees.

Intersectionality: Underrepresented leaders may face the cumulative effects of multiple forms of discrimination and marginalization due to their intersecting identities. For example, a leader who identifies as both a woman and a person of color may experience specific stressors related to gender and race simultaneously. Intersectional stressors can contribute to burnout. While specific studies on intersectionality and burnout among leaders are limited, research by McCallister et al. (2018) highlights the unique challenges intersectional individuals face in the workplace.

It is important to note that the research on burnout among underrepresented leaders is still emerging, and there may be variations based on specific contexts and industries. Further research is needed to provide more comprehensive statistics and specific comparisons between underrepresented leaders and white men in leadership.

Support Systems and Strategies: Building Resilient Teams

Resilient Leader Profile: Thasunda Brown Duckett - Empowering Financial Leader and Catalyst for Change

Thasunda Brown Duckett stands tall as an exemplar of resilience, embodying the transformative power of leadership and the indomitable human spirit. As a trailblazer in the financial industry, she has shattered barriers and redefined what it means to be a resilient leader, inspiring others with her unwavering determination, compassion, and commitment to empowering individuals from all walks of life.

From her humble beginnings in Texas, Duckett's journey to becoming a formidable force in the corporate world is a testament to her resilience.

Raised in a family that valued education and hard work, she cultivated a strong work ethic and an unwavering belief in the power of education to open doors. Armed with a degree from the University of Houston and an MBA from Baylor University, Duckett embarked on a path leading her to extraordinary achievements and groundbreaking leadership roles.

Duckett's rise to prominence occurred within the financial industry, where she quickly made a name for herself through her exceptional strategic acumen, vision, and ability to connect with people from diverse backgrounds. With her keen understanding of financial literacy and economic empowerment, she became a catalyst for change, dedicated to breaking down barriers and fostering economic equality.

As the former CEO of Chase Consumer Banking, Duckett spearheaded innovative initiatives to address the financial needs of underserved communities. Her tireless efforts to expand access to banking services, provide financial education, and support small businesses have profoundly impacted countless individuals and communities. Through her leadership, she has opened doors of opportunity, empowering individuals to take control of their financial futures and pursue their dreams.

Beyond her professional achievements, Duckett's resilience also shines through in her personal life. She has embraced her role as a wife and mother, navigating the complexities of work-life balance with grace and determination. Her ability to juggle multiple responsibilities while remaining steadfast in her commitment to serving others is a testament to her unwavering resilience and belief in the power of community and family.

Duckett's transformative leadership and unwavering commitment to equity and inclusion have earned her numerous accolades and recognition. Her inspiring journey and passion for empowering others have made her a sought-after speaker and advocate, amplifying the voices of underrepresented communities and championing diversity in leadership positions.

Thasunda Brown Duckett's story exemplifies the transformative power of resilience and leadership. Her unwavering dedication to empowering individuals and her strategic vision and compassionate approach have left an indelible mark on the financial industry and beyond. As a resilient leader, she reminds us all that it is not only our successes but also our ability to overcome challenges and lift others along the way that defines our true impact.

Thasunda Brown Duckett's legacy inspires aspiring leaders everywhere, urging them to embrace their unique strengths, champion inclusivity, and use their platforms to effect positive change. Through her unwavering resilience and relentless pursuit of empowerment and equality, she has set a powerful example for industry leaders, reminding us that we can shape a more equitable and prosperous future for all.

Chapter 7

INSPIRING HOPE: COMMUNICATING WITH IMPACT

Dear Resilient Leader,

Your presence as an individual who is dedicated to improving your environment fills me with optimism for the future. I can only believe that the excitement your presence inspires in me speaks to your potential to activate hope in others. In that spirit, hope is the concept I'd like to emphasize today. When you reinforce your own well-being, you strengthen your role as a cornerstone of hope for others. When you embody enduring leadership values, you leave an indelible mark on every space and person you encounter. Allow me to elaborate on some main ideas related to inspirational communication.

The Power of Hope: Motivating and Inspiring Others

In times of uncertainty, resilient leaders must harness the power of hope. Communicating a vision filled with optimism and possibility can ignite the motivation and drive within your team. You inspire your colleagues to persist through challenges and strive for success by illuminating the path ahead. Remember, your words have the potential to shape perspectives and instill unwavering belief in the collective journey.

Leading With a Growth Mindset: Creating Positive Work Boundaries

Resilient leaders understand the significance of adopting a growth mindset and encouraging their team members to do the same. By embracing a continuous learning mindset, you create an environment that promotes personal and professional growth. Cultivating a positive work-life balance is equally vital. By setting healthy boundaries and fostering a culture that supports self-care, you empower your team to maintain their well-being, ensuring they have the resilience to weather storms and bounce back stronger.

Embracing Fear: Inspiring Hope for Success and Growth

Fear can be a powerful force that holds individuals back, hindering their progress and stifling their potential. Resilient leaders recognize the importance of embracing fear and reframing it as an opportunity for growth. By openly discussing and acknowledging fears, you create a safe space for your team to address their concerns and move forward with courage. By sharing stories of your own experiences and lessons learned, you inspire hope, proving that success often emerges from the face of fear.

You become a beacon of hope for those you lead by nurturing your well-being and embodying these elements. Your words and actions hold the potential to inspire, motivate, and empower your team members to overcome challenges, embrace growth, and strive for success.

Remember, as a resilient leader, your impact extends beyond the immediate goals and objectives. Your leadership catalyzes transformation, both individually and collectively. Investing in your well-being, fostering growth mindsets, and embracing fear create a culture of hope and resilience that transcends limitations, propelling your team towards greater achievements.

Thank you for your unwavering dedication to making a positive difference in these challenging times. Your leadership is truly inspiring, and I am confident that by continuing to prioritize your own well-being, you will inspire hope and drive positive change within your team.

I wish you continued success and fulfillment on your leadership journey.

Best regards,

Jacqueline Twillie
Founder of ZeroGap.co
Creator of the Resilient Leaders Program

Jacqueline V. Twillie

THE POWER OF HOPE: MOTIVATING AND INSPIRING OTHERS

Hope is a remarkable and transformative force that can motivate and inspire individuals to achieve beyond their imagination. In times of uncertainty and adversity, resilient leaders understand the importance of cultivating hope within themselves and others. By fostering a culture of hope, leaders can ignite a sense of purpose, drive, and determination, propelling their teams to overcome challenges and achieve extraordinary results. In this section, we will explore the impact of hope and provide examples of how it can motivate and inspire others to reach their full potential.

Hope is a beacon of light during dark and challenging times. When leaders infuse their communication with hope, they instill a sense of belief within their teams, enabling them to persevere in adversity. Consider the example of a CEO leading a company through a financial crisis. The leader instills hope by openly acknowledging the challenges while expressing confidence in the team's ability to overcome them, encouraging employees to channel their energy into finding innovative solutions. This collective hope fuels determination and resilience, leading to the successful navigation of the crisis.

Hope provides a powerful framework for setting and achieving goals. When leaders articulate a compelling vision and share their belief in its attainability, they inspire hope within their teams. For instance, imagine a coach preparing their sports team for a crucial match. The coach instills hope and ignites a competitive spirit by consistently reinforcing the team's potential and expressing optimism about their ability to win. This hope motivates the team to work diligently, hone their skills, and surpass their expectations, ultimately leading to victory.

Hope fosters an environment of possibility and encourages individuals to think outside the box. When leaders cultivate hope, they create a space where innovative ideas flourish. Consider a scenario where a team faces a complex problem that seems insurmountable. A leader who inspires hope empowers team members to explore unconventional solutions and take calculated risks. The belief in a positive outcome fuels creativity, enabling the team to discover breakthrough approaches and generate transformative results.

Hope catalyzes resilience and enables individuals to bounce back from setbacks. Leaders who communicate hope during challenging times infuse their teams with optimism and determination. For example, a project manager leading a team through a project delay can inspire hope by emphasizing the lessons learned and the potential for future success. By fostering hope, the leader helps team members reframe setbacks as opportunities for growth, fueling resilience and inspiring them to continue striving for excellence.

Hope fosters a sense of unity and collaboration among team members. When leaders cultivate an atmosphere of hope, they promote trust, open communication, and a shared purpose. Imagine a leader launching a new initiative within an organization. By articulating a vision that highlights the collective impact and the positive change that can be achieved, the leader sparks hope within team members, encouraging collaboration and the pooling of diverse perspectives. This shared hope creates synergy and empowers the team to achieve extraordinary outcomes together.

Hope is a powerful force that can transform individuals, teams, and organizations. Resilient leaders understand their potential and purposefully cultivate hope to motivate and inspire others. By infusing their communication with hope, leaders enable individuals to overcome adversity, set and achieve ambitious goals, foster innovation and creativity, build resilience, and foster collaboration. As leaders embrace the power of hope, they become catalysts for positive change and create environments where individuals can flourish and reach their full potential.

Remember, in times of uncertainty, hope becomes the driving force that propels individuals and teams toward success and growth. As a resilient leader, embracing and sharing hope can create a lasting impact on those you lead, inspiring them to achieve greatness and surpass their expectations.

LEADING WITH GROWTH MINDSET: CREATING POSITIVE WORK BOUNDARIES

In the modern workplace, resilient leaders understand that leading with a growth mindset and creating positive work boundaries go hand in hand. A growth mindset fosters a culture of continuous learning, adaptability, and resilience, while positive work boundaries ensure a healthy work-life balance and promote overall well-being. This chapter explores the relationship between leading with a growth mindset and creating positive work boundaries, highlighting how these elements complement each other and contribute to a harmonious and productive work environment.

Positive work boundaries are essential for maintaining a healthy work-life balance and fostering employee well-being. Resilient leaders recognize the importance of establishing clear expectations, promoting self-care, and limiting work-related demands. By encouraging work-life integration and supporting employees' well-being, leaders create an environment that enhances productivity, job satisfaction, and overall mental and physical health. Positive work boundaries also foster a sense of trust, autonomy, and responsibility among team members.

Combining a growth mindset and positive work boundaries creates an environment of psychological safety. Resilient leaders encourage open communication, active listening, and constructive feedback, which allows employees to voice their opinions, share ideas, and express concerns without fear of judgment or retribution. When individuals feel psychologically safe, they are more willing to take risks, innovate, and contribute their best work. This, in turn, promotes collaboration, creativity, and collective growth within the team.

A growth mindset and positive work boundaries strengthen leaders' and their teams' resilience and adaptability. By fostering a culture that embraces challenges, values continuous learning, and encourages self-care, leaders enable individuals to bounce back from setbacks, navigate change effectively, and maintain their well-being in adversity. This promotes a resilient workforce that can adapt to evolving circumstances, innovate, and thrive even in the most challenging situations.

Leaders who prioritize both a growth mindset and positive work boundaries create opportunities for the growth and development of their team members. They provide resources, mentorship, and growth-oriented feedback that help individuals reach their full potential. By offering guidance, recognizing achievements, and empowering employees to take ownership of their professional growth, leaders foster a sense of purpose and motivation within their teams. This leads to increased job satisfaction, employee engagement, and long-term success.

Leading with a growth mindset and creating positive work boundaries are interconnected practices that amplify each other's impact. A growth mindset cultivates a culture of continuous learning, adaptability, and innovation, while positive work boundaries promote well-being, work-life balance, and psychological safety. Combined, these elements contribute to a thriving and productive work environment, fostering resilience, enhancing employee engagement, and enabling individuals and teams to reach their full potential. Resilient leaders who embrace a growth mindset and establish positive work boundaries create a foundation for success, growth, and sustainable excellence in today's dynamic and fast-paced workplaces.

Resilient Leader Profile: Nedra Glover Tawwab

Nedra Glover Tawwab is a leader who has significantly impacted mental health and personal development. As a licensed therapist, writer, and speaker, Tawwab has dedicated her career to helping individuals foster healthier relationships with themselves and others. Her resilience, compassion, and commitment to personal growth make her an inspiring role model for leaders worldwide.

As a highly sought-after therapist and relationship expert, Tawwab possesses deep knowledge and expertise in emotional wellness. She has empowered countless individuals to navigate challenging emotions, set healthy boundaries, and cultivate self-awareness through her work. Tawwab's ability to provide practical and cultural guidance with compassionate support has made her a trusted resource in the mental health community.

One of the defining qualities of Tawwab's leadership is her unwavering compassion and empathy speaking in language that empowers people to be honest about their mental health journey. She understands the importance of meeting individuals where they are, and she creates a safe and inclusive space for vulnerability and growth. Tawwab's empathetic approach allows her to foster trust and provide the support necessary for personal transformation in written, audio, and video messages.

She actively engages in ongoing learning, research, and professional development to stay at the forefront of her field. By demonstrating a commitment to her own growth, Tawwab inspires others to embark on their own journeys of self-discovery and improvement.

As mentioned earlier, through her writing and speaking engagements, Tawwab has become a thought leader and advocate for mental health. Her candid and authentic approach to addressing boundaries, self-worth, and emotional well-being has resonated with a broad audience, inspiring positive change and fostering a sense of hope.

Tawwab's resilience is evident in her overcoming personal and professional challenges. She has openly shared her own experiences of growth and healing, demonstrating that resilience is not about avoiding difficulties but rather about facing them head-on. Tawwab's ability to navigate adversity with grace and determination is a powerful example for others, illustrating the transformative power of resilience.

Nedra embodies the qualities of a resilient leader who has impacted mental health and personal development. Her expertise, compassion, commitment to personal growth, thought leadership, and resilience inspire individuals to embrace their own journeys of healing and self-improvement. If you haven't had a chance to dive into her work, I encourage you to add it to your reading list. She is a role model for leaders everywhere, demonstrating that resilience, empathy, and a dedication to personal growth can lead to profound positive change.

EMBRACING FEAR: INSPIRING HOPE FOR SUCCESS AND GROWTH

In the quest for success and growth, resilient leaders understand that fear can paralyze or propel individuals and teams forward. By embracing fear and transforming it into a catalyst for positive change, leaders can inspire hope, foster resilience, and create an environment conducive to success and growth. In this section, we will explore the power of embracing fear and the quote from the Resilient Leader Manifesto to inspire hope and drive success in the face of uncertainty and challenges.

> *Embracing change: We embrace change as an opportunity to grow, adapt, and evolve. We are not fearless yet; instead, we welcome fear and determine the wisest path in taking risks and embracing new ideas, even when uncertain or unpopular.*

Fear is a natural response to uncertainty and unfamiliar situations. Resilient leaders acknowledge fear as a catalyst for growth rather than an obstacle to success. They understand that great achievements often require stepping outside their comfort zones, taking risks, and embracing change. By reframing fear as an indicator of growth potential, leaders inspire hope and motivate individuals and teams to face challenges with courage and determination.

Embracing fear as a resilient leader means creating an environment where hope thrives despite uncertainty. When leaders acknowledge their fears and openly communicate about them, they humanize the experience, fostering a sense of connection and empathy within the team. Leaders inspire hope by sharing stories of overcoming fear, highlighting the potential rewards of taking calculated risks, and igniting a collective belief in the possibilities beyond fear.

Resilient leaders create a culture of psychological safety where team members feel supported and empowered to take risks without fear of judgment or punishment. They encourage open dialogue, active listening, and constructive feedback, allowing individuals to express their concerns, ideas, and fears freely. This inclusive and non-judgmental environment fosters trust and collaboration, enabling individuals to confront and conquer their fears together, inspiring hope, and driving success.

Embracing fear involves leveraging it as a catalyst for personal and professional growth. Resilient leaders encourage individuals to confront their fears, embrace new challenges, and push their boundaries. They provide resources, mentorship, and guidance to help team members navigate fear, supporting them in developing the skills and mindset necessary for growth. By transforming fear into growth opportunities, leaders inspire hope and cultivate a culture of continuous improvement and resilience.

The quote from the Resilient Leader Manifesto emphasizes embracing change as an opportunity for growth and evolution. Resilient leaders understand that change is inevitable and necessary for progress. They encourage individuals to embrace change, adopt a growth mindset, and welcome new ideas even when uncertainty or opposition arises. Leaders inspire hope, encourage creative problem-solving, and drive success in a rapidly evolving world by fostering a culture that celebrates innovation and adaptability.

Embracing fear is a powerful mindset that resilient leaders adopt to inspire hope, drive success, and foster growth in themselves and their teams. By acknowledging fear as a catalyst, cultivating a culture of psychological safety, and turning fear into growth opportunities, leaders create an environment where individuals are empowered to confront challenges, take risks, and achieve remarkable outcomes. Through the quote from the Resilient Leader Manifesto, leaders emphasize the importance of embracing change, demonstrating that by welcoming fear and determining the wisest path, hope is ignited, and success and growth are within reach.

Chapter 8

RISK, RESILIENCE & REWARD: EMBRACING CHALLENGES FOR GROWTH

Dear Resilient Leader,

I hope this email finds you well, navigating the dynamic business landscape with determination and adaptability. As we continue to encounter various challenges, I wanted to take a moment to reflect on the importance of risk, resilience, and the ultimate rewards they can bring.

Calculated risks are an inherent part of achieving meaningful growth. However, the ability to embrace these risks and transform them into opportunities requires a resilient mindset. It is this very resilience that sets great leaders apart and enables them to weather storms and emerge stronger.

To calculate risk, we must begin by assessing the potential outcomes of a particular decision or action. By analyzing the probability of each outcome and considering the potential impact, we can estimate the overall risk involved. Various techniques, such as quantitative models and qualitative assessments, can assist in this process. It is crucial to gather relevant data and insights, consult subject matter experts, and leverage historical data to make informed decisions.

When we successfully navigate risks with resilience, we open ourselves up to a world of potential rewards. These rewards may come in various forms, including financial gains, increased market share, improved brand reputation, and personal growth. In whatever form they come, don't forget to celebrate the way life rewards you for the chances you take.

My wish for you today is that every risk you take is well-informed—and then rewarded beyond your wildest imagination.

Best regards,

Jacqueline V. Twillie
Founder of ZeroGap.co
Creator of the Resilient Leaders Program

CALCULATED RISKS: BALANCING AMBITION AND PRUDENCE

Taking risks is essential to a fulfilling career, but not all risks are equal. Some risks can lead to career growth and success, while others can harm your career and well-being. Navigating healthy and unhealthy risks can be incredibly challenging for underrepresented leaders in male-dominated industries. Here's what you need to know:

Healthy risks involve taking calculated, strategic risks that align with your career goals and values. These risks include taking on new challenges, pursuing higher education or training, or seeking a mentor or sponsor. Healthy risks can help you build skills, gain experience, and advance your career.

Here are 10 examples of healthy career risks for leaders:

1. Taking on a leadership role in a new project or initiative with high visibility.
2. Pursuing a new certification or degree to expand your skill set and knowledge while balancing home responsibilities.
3. Seeking out a mentor or sponsor to provide guidance and support when rejection is a possibility.
4. Taking on a new role in a different department or organization to gain new experiences.
5. Speaking up and advocating for yourself and your team in a challenging situation.
6. Starting a new project or initiative that aligns with your values and career goals.
7. Pursuing a career change to a new industry or field that aligns better with your passions and interests.
8. Networking with new professionals and attending industry events to expand your network.

9. Negotiating for a higher salary or better benefits package that aligns with your worth and career goals.
10. Taking a sabbatical or extended break to recharge and gain a new perspective.

Unhealthy risks, on the other hand, involve taking risks that are impulsive, reckless, or that go against your values or priorities. These risks include staying in a toxic work environment, burning bridges with colleagues, or compromising your ethics. Unhealthy risks can lead to stress, burnout, and a damaged reputation.

Here are some examples of unhealthy career risks:

- Staying in a toxic work environment negatively impacts your mental health and well-being.
- Compromising your ethics or values for the sake of career advancement.
- Burning bridges with colleagues or damaging professional relationships.
- Taking on too many responsibilities or projects leads to burnout and stress.
- Refusing to seek help or support when struggling with a challenging situation.
- Neglecting your personal life and relationships for the sake of work.
- Failing to seek out professional development or training opportunities.
- Refusing to adapt to new technologies or systems hindering your ability to grow and advance.
- Not setting boundaries or saying no to unreasonable demands, leading to overwhelm and stress.
- Failing to seek feedback or constructive criticism to improve your performance and skills.

The pressure to take risks can be exceptionally high for underrepresented leaders in male-dominated industries. However, it's important to remember that not all risks are worth taking. As an underrepresented leader, assessing your risks and ensuring they align with your values and priorities is essential. This may involve seeking out mentorship, building a support network, and staying true to your authentic self.

Navigating healthy and unhealthy risks is essential for a fulfilling career, especially for underrepresented leaders in male-dominated industries. Taking calculated and strategic risks that align with your values and priorities can build skills, gain experience, and advance your career. At the same time, it's essential to recognize and avoid unhealthy risks that can lead to stress, burnout, and a damaged reputation. By leveraging your strengths, building resilience, and staying true to yourself, you can navigate risks and build a successful and fulfilling career.

Resilient Leader Profile: Rosalind Brewer

Rosalind Brewer is a remarkable leader who has consistently demonstrated resilience and determination throughout her illustrious career. As a prominent organization's Chief Executive Officer, she has achieved impressive professional milestones. Still, she has also become influential, inspiring others to embrace resilience and strive for excellence.

Rosalind Brewer's journey to becoming a resilient leader is a testament to her unwavering commitment to personal growth and adaptability. From the beginning of her career, she displayed exceptional leadership skills and an ability to navigate challenges with grace and determination. Her strong work ethic and dedication propelled her into various leadership roles within the organization.

Throughout her career, Rosalind Brewer encountered numerous obstacles and faced adversity head-on. She confronted gender and racial biases, breaking barriers and paving the way for future generations. Despite facing these challenges, she remained steadfast in her pursuit of success and used these experiences as opportunities to foster resilience within herself and others.

Rosalind Brewer understands that change is inevitable in the corporate landscape. She consistently seeks innovative solutions and proactively adapts to emerging trends, staying ahead of the curve. By embracing change, she has created an organizational culture that encourages continuous learning, growth, and resilience.

As a resilient leader, Rosalind Brewer leads by example and inspires her team to rise above challenges. She fosters an inclusive and collaborative work environment where diverse perspectives are valued. Her exceptional communication skills allow her to effectively articulate her vision, motivate her team, and rally them around a common purpose, empowering them to reach their full potential.

Rosalind Brewer's resilience extends beyond the boardroom. She is deeply committed to making a positive impact on society. Through various philanthropic initiatives and partnerships, she actively works towards creating opportunities for underrepresented communities and promoting diversity and inclusion on a broader scale.

Rosalind Brewer's legacy as a resilient leader will undoubtedly leave a lasting impact. Her ability to navigate challenges, embrace change, and inspire others to overcome adversity has set a powerful example for aspiring leaders. Through her leadership, she has achieved remarkable success and created a pathway for others to follow.

Rosalind Brewer exemplifies what it means to be a resilient leader. Her unwavering determination, ability to embrace change, and commitment to empowering others have propelled her to the forefront of her industry. As a trailblazer and advocate for diversity and inclusion, she has left an indelible mark on the corporate world, inspiring current and future leaders to unlock their power of resilience and achieve extraordinary success.

RESILIENCE IN THE FACE OF CHALLENGES: OVERCOMING OBSTACLES FOR REWARD

Rewards of Being Resilient

Leadership allows for mental clarity when navigating the complex and ever-changing landscape of challenges, including market conditions, challenges with personalities, and scope of work changes. Resilient leaders remain steadfast and adaptable despite adversity. They understand market conditions are dynamic and proactively adjust strategies to stay competitive. When faced with challenges stemming from diverse personalities, resilient leaders cultivate solid emotional intelligence, fostering positive relationships and effectively managing conflicts. Moreover, they embrace the fluidity of work scope changes, swiftly identifying opportunities within them and guiding their teams through transitions. Resilient leaders inspire confidence, promote innovation, and create a resilient organizational culture that not only withstands challenges but thrives in the midst of them. As we've discussed in this book, being a resilient leader is the ability to adapt to change and overcome challenges, and it's a valuable trait to have in life; equally as important is understanding how to determine the rewards of being resilient:

Mental health is a vital aspect of overall well-being, and resilience plays a significant role in maintaining and improving it. As you continue to develop resiliency, you gain the ability to manage stress effectively and bounce back from adversity, leading to enhanced mental health. Resilient leaders are better equipped to handle the pressures and challenges of life, as they possess the capacity to adapt, problem-solve, and maintain a positive mindset in the face of adversity. This allows you to cope with stressful situations more effectively, reducing the negative impact on your mental health. Moreover, resilience fosters a sense of empowerment and self-efficacy, enabling individuals to approach challenges with confidence and optimism and promoting better mental well-being. Overall, cultivating resilience improves mental health by providing leaders with the skills and mindset necessary to navigate life's ups and downs with resilience and strength.

Unpacking the physical health benefits of cultivating resilience reveals a multitude of advantages. When an individual develops resilience, they can handle stress more effectively. This enhanced capacity to cope with life's challenges can significantly lower the risk of developing various health problems. By managing stress, resilience reduces ailments such as high blood pressure, heart disease, and depression. The ability to navigate stressful situations with composure and adaptability creates a healthier physiological response within the body, resulting in improved overall well-being. Thus, fostering resilience acts as a shield, safeguarding against the potential negative impacts of stress on physical health.

One notable benefit of resilience is the positive impact it has on self-esteem. When leaders cultivate resilience, they tap into the growth mindset and perceive challenges as valuable personal growth and development opportunities. Rather than feeling overwhelmed or defeated by setbacks, they view them as chances to learn, adapt, and improve. The practice of resilience is a continual process and should be activated as necessary when navigating challenges. This shift in mindset fosters a sense of empowerment and confidence as individuals recognize their ability to overcome obstacles and bounce back from adversity. By embracing challenges with resilience, leaders build a strong belief in their capabilities, contributing to increased self-esteem and a greater sense of self-worth.

This heightened self-assurance enhances their overall well-being and enables them to approach future challenges with resilience and optimism.

Conflict and challenges can be easily managed, ultimately fostering healthier and more fulfilling workplace relationships. Leaders who possess resilience are better equipped to manage conflicts with others constructively and productively. They approach disagreements or differing opinions with empathy, open-mindedness, and a focus on finding mutually beneficial solutions. Resilient leaders can navigate challenging situations by maintaining composure and emotional stability without resorting to destructive behaviors or damaging relationships. Moreover, their ability to bounce back from setbacks and adapt to change instills confidence and trust among team members, leading to a more positive work environment. The awareness of resilient leaders cultivates a culture of resilience within the workplace, encouraging others to handle conflicts and challenges healthily and collaboratively. This, in turn, leads to stronger relationships, improved communication, and, ultimately, a more cohesive and successful team dynamic.

Another significant reward of resilience in leadership is the development of additional pathways to problem-solving. Leaders who cultivate resilience adopt a solution-focused mindset when faced with challenges. Instead of becoming overwhelmed or fixated on the problem, resilient leaders view challenges as opportunities for growth and learning. This perspective enables them to approach problems creatively and resourcefully, seeking innovative solutions. By embracing adversity and maintaining a positive outlook, resilient leaders are more likely to think vitally, analyze situations from various angles, and explore unconventional approaches. As a result, they develop strong problem-solving skills that enable them to overcome obstacles effectively and find successful resolutions. The ability to adapt and find creative solutions enhances the leader's effectiveness and inspires and empowers team members to approach problems similarly, fostering a culture of innovation and continuous improvement.

The rewards of resilience are abundant, and concluding this section without highlighting career success and happiness would be incomplete. First, increased career success is a notable outcome of resilience. As individuals develop resilience, they become better equipped to handle daily stressors within their jobs. Consciously cultivating a resilient mindset, leaders navigate setbacks, adapt to changes, and persevere in unpredictable circumstances. This ability enhances job satisfaction and paves the way for business units to achieve their goals. Resilient leaders demonstrate a strong work ethic, problem-solving skills, and the ability to bounce back from failures, all contributing to their professional growth and fulfillment. Second, resilience significantly impacts one's happiness and overall life satisfaction. By approaching challenges with a growth and resilient mindset, leaders maintain emotional well-being and find satisfaction in their daily lives. Resilience becomes a conscious habit when coping with stress, bouncing back from setbacks, and embracing change, leading to greater happiness, contentment, and overall life satisfaction.

Devoting time and effort to elevate your attention and intention on resilience may require dedication, but the rewards are undoubtedly worthwhile. Developing resilience involves a deliberate focus on various aspects. First and foremost, prioritizing self-care is essential. Taking care of your physical, emotional, and mental well-being provides a solid foundation for resilience. Additionally, seeking support from mentors and coaches who can provide guidance, wisdom, and encouragement can greatly enhance your resilience-building journey. Finally, practicing growth mindset principles, such as embracing challenges, learning from setbacks, and fostering a belief in your ability to grow and improve, is instrumental in cultivating resilience. By incorporating these strategies into your life, you will gradually nurture and strengthen your resilience, paving the way for personal growth, increased well-being, and the ability to face life's challenges with greater fortitude.

Take time to reflect on the situation in which you took a risk. Consider what went well, what didn't go as planned, and what you learned from the experience.

It's normal to feel a range of emotions after taking risks, such as disappointment, frustration, or relief. Take the time to acknowledge and process these emotions. This may involve talking to someone you trust, journaling, or practicing self-care.

Once you have processed your emotions and reflected on the experience, it's time to create a plan. This may involve setting new goals, developing new strategies, or finding new opportunities to take risks.

Remember to celebrate your successes, big or small. Celebrating your accomplishments will help you stay motivated and focused on your goals.

Resetting, being resilient, and achieving rewards after taking risks is an ongoing cycle. Keep repeating this process as you take risks and pursue your goals.

Taking risks can be challenging, but you can reset, be resilient, and achieve rewards with the right mindset and approach.

The risk of not taking a risk is often missing out on opportunities for growth and advancement. When we avoid taking risks, we limit our potential for success and the possibility of discovering new experiences and ideas. Failing to take risks can result in missed chances to develop new skills, build confidence, and challenge ourselves.

On the other hand, not taking risks can also have some benefits. For example, it can reduce stress, minimize the potential for failure or loss, and provide stability and security. However, balancing taking calculated risks and avoiding unnecessary or foolish risks is vital.

Not taking risks can have negative and positive consequences, and it's up to each individual to determine the right level of risk based on their goals, values, and personal circumstances.

CELEBRATING SUCCESS: ACKNOWLEDGING AND EMBRACING THE REWARDS OF RESILIENCE

Success culminates in intentional work, perseverance, and resilience. It is important to recognize and celebrate our achievements, both big and small, as it reinforces our sense of accomplishment and motivates us to strive for more. This guide aims to provide valuable insights and practical tips on acknowledging and embracing the rewards of resilience. Let's dive in and discover how to celebrate success meaningfully and meaningfully.

Take a moment to reflect on the path you've traveled and acknowledge the obstacles you've overcome. Recognize the difficulties you've encountered, the setbacks you've faced, and the wisdom you've gained. This introspection will help you recognize the significance of your achievements and the personal development you've undergone.

Mark your successes by setting objectives and establishing milestones. Breaking down your larger goals into smaller, attainable tasks enables you to monitor your progress and acknowledge the milestones you reach. Each milestone reached is a cause for celebration, granting you a sense of fulfillment and bolstering your drive.

Expressing gratitude is a powerful means of commemorating success. Take the time to convey your appreciation to those who supported and believed in you throughout your journey. This could include friends, family, mentors, colleagues, or yourself. Cultivating gratitude strengthens your relationships and deepens your overall well-being, fostering a genuine appreciation for the fruits of your resilience.

Don't delay celebrating until you've achieved your ultimate goal. Embrace the rewards of your perseverance by rejoicing in the small victories along the way. Acknowledge and reward yourself for each step forward, no matter how seemingly insignificant. Treat yourself to a small indulgence, spend quality time with loved ones, or engage in activities that bring you joy. These celebrations will uplift your spirits and sustain your motivation.

Sharing your tale of triumph enables you to celebrate your accomplishments while inspiring and motivating others. Speak of your journey, the obstacles you confronted, and the strategies you employed to surmount them. By sharing your story, you can offer valuable insights and lessons learned to those undergoing similar struggles, creating a positive impact and reinforcing your success.

Surround yourself with a supportive network of individuals who celebrate your achievements and uplift you during difficult times. Engage with communities, join professional networks, or seek mentors who can provide guidance and encouragement. Celebrating success becomes even more meaningful when shared with others who comprehend and value your journey.

Success is about celebrating the result and learning from the process. Take the time to reflect on your successes and failures, identify areas of improvement, and set new goals. Continuous learning and growth are essential to celebrating success and embracing the rewards of resilience.

Celebrating success is a momentary event and a continuous journey that allows us to acknowledge and embrace the rewards of resilience. By reflecting on our journey, setting clear goals, expressing gratitude, celebrating small wins, sharing our success stories, cultivating a supportive network, and embracing continuous learning, we can truly celebrate our achievements meaningfully and fulfillingly. So, go ahead, embrace your resilience, and celebrate the success you have earned!

Chapter 9

BUILDING TRUST & VISION SETTING: CREATING A FOUNDATION FOR SUCCESS

Dear Resilient Leader,

I hope this message finds you well. I wanted to emphasize the importance of trust and a compelling vision in effective leadership. These two elements are the bedrock for success, enabling your team to collaborate and accomplish remarkable outcomes.

Trust plays a pivotal role in fostering strong relationships and promoting collaboration. As a leader, leading with honesty, open and transparent communication, and a genuine willingness to listen to your team is crucial. Uphold your commitments, respect confidentiality, and ensure fairness in decision-making processes.

Equally important is setting a clear and inspiring vision that motivates your team. Involve them in shaping the vision, communicate it with clarity and enthusiasm, and emphasize their integral role in its achievement. Regularly reinforce the vision and celebrate milestones that mark progress along the way.

By prioritizing trust and vision, you establish a solid foundation for your team's success.

Nurture trust, foster open communication, and actively engage your team in shaping and realizing the vision.

I wish you the joy of seeing your greatest visions come alive before your eyes. I am confident that day is coming soon.

Best regards,

Jacqueline Twillie
Founder of ZeroGap.co
Creator of the Resilient Leaders Program

THE IMPORTANCE OF TRUST: BUILDING AND CULTIVATING STRONG TEAM RELATIONSHIPS

Trust forms the cornerstone of strong team relationships and plays a vital role in fostering collaboration, productivity, and success within any organization. In this section, we will explore six key areas that highlight the significance of trust in building and cultivating strong team relationships.

Trust is the linchpin of effective communication within teams. When team members trust one another, they feel comfortable openly sharing their thoughts, ideas, and concerns. This fosters a transparent and collaborative environment where information flows freely, leading to better decision-making and problem-solving.

Trust encourages collaboration and cooperation among team members. When trust exists, individuals are more willing to seek help, offer assistance, and work together towards common goals. This collaboration results in increased synergy, productivity, and innovative thinking, as team members feel safe to share their expertise and perspectives.

Team members are more engaged and motivated in a high-trust environment, increasing productivity. When individuals trust their colleagues, they are more likely to delegate tasks, rely on each other's abilities, and work efficiently as a cohesive unit. This trust-driven productivity enhances team performance and paves the way for exceptional results.

Trust creates a psychological safety net that encourages team members to take risks and think creatively. When individuals feel trusted and supported, they are more inclined to share bold ideas, challenge the status quo, and explore innovative solutions. This environment of trust fosters a culture of continuous learning, experimentation, and growth, propelling the team toward success.

Trust is the foundation of strong interpersonal relationships within teams. It nurtures mutual respect, empathy, and understanding among team members. When trust exists, conflicts can be resolved constructively, and differences in opinions can be openly discussed. This cultivates a positive and harmonious team dynamic, where individuals value and appreciate each other's contributions.

Trust plays a crucial role in employee engagement and retention. When team members trust their leaders and colleagues, they feel more connected to the organization and its goals. This sense of belonging and loyalty leads to higher job satisfaction, increased commitment, and reduced turnover rates. Trust-based relationships create an environment where individuals feel valued, supported, and motivated to give their best.

Trust is a fundamental ingredient in building and cultivating strong team relationships. It enhances communication, promotes collaboration, boosts productivity, fosters innovation, builds strong interpersonal connections, and enhances employee engagement and retention. As a leader, investing time and effort in establishing and nurturing trust within your team can yield immense benefits, driving the team toward success and achieving remarkable outcomes.

IMAGINATION TO VISION: ALIGNING ACTION

Imagination and vision are powerful forces that drive innovation, transformation, and progress. When harnessed effectively, they have the potential to inspire and align actions toward the realization of extraordinary goals.

Imagination catalyzes envisioning new possibilities and thinking beyond the current boundaries. It allows us to tap into our creativity and explore innovative ideas that have the potential to reshape the future. By encouraging imaginative thinking, individuals and organizations can generate fresh perspectives and break free from conventional constraints.

Imagination alone is not enough; it must be translated into a compelling vision. A vision is a guiding light, providing a clear direction and purpose for individuals and teams. It encapsulates the desired future state and defines an organization's goals, values, and aspirations. Turning imagination into a vision involves distilling the essence of imaginative ideas into a concise and inspiring statement that captures the hearts and minds of all involved.

A vision is only effective if it is communicated effectively. Leaders must articulate the vision in a way that resonates with the team, inspiring them to align their actions and efforts toward its realization. Through compelling storytelling, visual aids, and consistent messaging, leaders can create a shared understanding and enthusiasm around the vision, fostering a sense of collective ownership.

To bring the vision to life, aligning actions and strategies with the overarching goal is crucial. This involves breaking down the vision into actionable steps, setting measurable objectives, and developing a roadmap to guide the journey. Leaders must ensure that every team member understands their role in achieving the vision and provide the necessary resources and support to facilitate their success. Regular check-ins, feedback loops, and course corrections are vital to aligning the actions with the evolving vision.

Aligning action with the vision requires cultivating a culture of innovation and continuous improvement. Encouraging and rewarding experimentation, risk-taking, and learning from failures enables individuals to explore new avenues and find creative solutions. By fostering a supportive environment that values and encourages diverse perspectives, organizations can harness the collective intelligence of their teams to drive progress toward the vision.

A vision is not static but evolves as circumstances change. Leaders must remain flexible and adaptable, willing to revise and refine the vision based on feedback, market dynamics, and emerging opportunities. Regularly revisiting the vision and aligning actions accordingly ensures that the organization stays on course and maintains relevance in a rapidly evolving landscape.

Imagination can shape our world, and transforming it into a clear vision is the first step toward achieving remarkable outcomes. By effectively communicating the vision and aligning actions, organizations can unleash the collective potential of their teams. Through a culture of innovation, adaptability, and continuous improvement, they can turn imagination into reality, driving progress and making a lasting impact. Embrace the power of imagination, craft a compelling vision, and align actions to create a future that surpasses your wildest dreams.

EMULATING EXCELLENCE: ADJUSTING VISION AND FOSTERING CONTINUOUS VALUES ALIGNMENT

Emulating excellence is a concept that emphasizes the importance of striving for personal best rather than chasing perfection. I had this idea in my early books, urging leaders to set an intention to give 110% daily. This section explores the concept of emulating excellence, highlighting the significance of adjusting vision and fostering continuous values alignment as key components of this approach.

The pursuit of perfection can be exhausting and unattainable. Emulating excellence shifts the focus to consistent personal bests, recognizing that true excellence comes from committing to continuous improvement and growth. By embracing emulating excellence, leaders can adopt a healthier, more sustainable approach to their work.

To emulate excellence, leaders must adjust their vision to align with continuous improvement and growth values. Instead of rigid and unattainable goals, leaders should create a vision encouraging ongoing development, learning, and innovation. This adaptive vision allows for flexibility and enables leaders and their teams to respond effectively to changing circumstances.

Values alignment is crucial in emulating excellence. Leaders and teams share common values centered on growth, integrity, and resilience, creating a cohesive and collaborative work environment. By consistently reinforcing and modeling these values, leaders establish a culture that supports continuous improvement and inspires individuals to give their best efforts each day.

Emulating excellence requires a commitment to continuous learning and development. Resilient leaders actively seek opportunities to expand their knowledge, refine their skills, and stay updated on industry trends. They encourage their teams to do the same, providing resources and support for professional growth. In this way, the best leaders embolden themselves and others to constantly learn and improve over time without equating success with achieving superhuman ideals.

Recognizing and celebrating progress and milestones is integral to emulating excellence. Resilient leaders understand the importance of acknowledging and appreciating individual and team achievements, regardless of scale. Celebrating milestones not only boosts morale but also reinforces the values of continuous improvement and motivates individuals to maintain their commitment to excellence.

Emulating excellence is a transformative approach to leadership that encourages resilient leaders to give their personal best each day. Leaders create a culture that supports and encourages excellence by adjusting their vision, fostering continuous values alignment, cultivating a growth mindset, embracing continuous learning, and celebrating progress. Emulating excellence acknowledges the imperfection inherent in the human experience while inspiring leaders and their teams to strive for continuous improvement, growth, and remarkable achievements.

Resilient Leader Profile: Thasunda Brown Duckett

We've already discussed the achievements of Thasunda Brown Duckett in Chapter 6, but it is worth highlighting her again in the context of the themes we're discussing in Chapter 9. She is an exceptional leader known for her resilience, commitment to excellence, and ability to let go of perfectionism. Throughout her career, she has demonstrated remarkable leadership skills, inspiring others to embrace their strengths, learn from failures, and cultivate a culture of continuous growth. This profile delves into Thasunda Brown Duckett's leadership qualities, focusing on her pursuit of excellence and her willingness to relinquish the constraints of perfectionism.

One of Thasunda Brown Duckett's defining characteristics is her resilience. She has faced numerous challenges throughout her professional journey, but rather than being deterred by setbacks, she has consistently bounced back stronger and more determined than before. This resilience has enabled her to adapt to changing circumstances, embrace new opportunities, and lead with unwavering determination. Thasunda understands that failure is an integral part of the learning process and has used setbacks as stepping stones for personal and professional growth.

Thasunda Brown Duckett's commitment to excellence is evident in everything she does. She sets high standards for herself and her team, always striving for the best possible outcomes. However, what sets her apart is her ability to inspire and empower others to achieve excellence. She understands that true success is not achieved in isolation. Still, through collaborative efforts and collective excellence. Thasunda fosters a culture of continuous improvement by encouraging her team to embrace a growth mindset, seek feedback, and consistently challenge themselves to reach higher levels of achievement.

While many leaders succumb to the pressures of perfectionism, Thasunda Brown Duckett recognizes its limitations. She understands that pursuing perfection can stifle creativity, hinder progress, and create unnecessary stress. Instead, she encourages her team to focus on progress over perfection, emphasizing the importance of taking risks, embracing innovation, and learning from failures. By letting go of the need for perfection, Thasunda creates an environment where individuals feel empowered to explore new ideas and pursue excellence without the fear of judgment or failure.

Thasunda Brown Duckett believes that resilient teams are the cornerstone of success. She invests in her team members' growth and development, providing them with the tools and resources necessary to excel in their roles. Thasunda fosters a sense of psychological safety, ensuring team members feel comfortable taking risks, sharing their ideas, and learning from successes and failures. By cultivating an environment that values growth and resilience, she inspires her team to reach their full potential, collectively achieving outstanding results.

Thasunda Brown Duckett is a remarkable leader who exemplifies resilience, excellence, and the ability to let go of perfectionism. Her unwavering determination in the face of challenges, commitment to continuous improvement, and emphasis on building resilient teams have earned her admiration and respect. Thasunda's leadership style serves as an inspiration for aspiring leaders, encouraging them to prioritize excellence, embrace failure as a learning opportunity, and foster environments where individuals can thrive and grow. By emulating Thasunda Brown Duckett's leadership qualities, one can pave the way for personal and professional success while fostering a culture of resilience and excellence.

Chapter 10

BUSINESS & PERSONAL NEGOTIATION: ADVOCATING FOR SUCCESS

Dear Resilient Leader,

I want to impress upon you a very important truth: Whether you intend it or not, you are a beacon of inspiration in your professional and personal spheres. Your colleagues, mentees, and community may not always say this outright, but it is true nonetheless. Whenever you use your voice to speak up for yourself and what you believe in, you are shedding light on a way forward for others. I urge you to embrace this role consciously. Leadership, at its core, is about being an advocate. That is, advocating for yourself and those you lead. As an advocate, you will need to sharpen your skills of negotiation so you can be a formidable champion at every level of the business world.

At various stages of your career, you will find that there are some challenges you cannot overcome through the force of determination or creativity alone. You will need support, and you will need more resources to get the job done. In those times, you will be faced with the task of fighting for what you need and deserve. The process of rebounding from adversities becomes more attainable when you and your organization are equipped with the proper tools and bolstered by a support system. This requires negotiation and may take weeks or even months to achieve, but it is a necessary part of successful leadership

Realizing your vision—whether it be a new venture, a new position, a plan for growth, or pushing your team to new heights—will require more than just a dream but also a sharp eye for the provisions needed to make it a reality. How do you construct a compelling business proposal to procure these resources? What negotiation strategy should you use to seal the deal? My recommendation is to use the L.A.T.T.E. negotiation framework to build the case to ask for what you need.

Whenever you leave the bargaining table, may you lead with your head held high.

Best regards,

Jacqueline V. Twillie
Founder of ZeroGap.co
Creator of the Resilient Leaders Program

INTRODUCING THE L.A.T.T.E. NEGOTIATION FRAMEWORK

In today's competitive business landscape, resilient leaders in male-dominated industries face unique challenges when it comes to negotiating both in their personal and professional lives. In my last book, *Don't Leave Money on the Table: Negotiation Strategies*, I delve into the intricacies of advocating for success in such environments. Drawing upon the concepts explored in my earlier book, this section of *Dear Resilient Leaders* highlights the relevance of the L.A.T.T.E. negotiation framework for resilient leaders seeking to overcome barriers and achieve favorable outcomes.

The L.A.T.T.E. negotiation framework, a key strategy discussed in my book, emphasizes the importance of leveraging the power of relationships and understanding the interests of all parties involved. Resilient leaders in male-dominated industries can use this framework to build rapport and establish credibility, fostering an environment of trust and respect during negotiations. Leaders can effectively navigate challenging conversations and reach mutually beneficial agreements by focusing on shared interests rather than fixed positions.

One of the key challenges resilient leaders face in male-dominated industries is the tendency for their voices to be overshadowed or dismissed. The L.A.T.T.E. negotiation framework encourages leaders to advocate assertively for themselves and their ideas. By highlighting their unique perspectives and demonstrating their value, unapologetically, they can assert their influence and contribute meaningfully to the negotiation process. This strategy empowers leaders to challenge traditional power dynamics and level the playing field, ultimately increasing their chances of success.

In addition to addressing workplace negotiations, the L.A.T.T.E. negotiation framework applies equally to personal negotiations for resilient leaders. Racial and gender biases and stereotypes often seep into personal relationships, influencing how individuals are perceived and treated. By using the latte negotiation framework, leaders can proactively address these biases and negotiate for equitable treatment and opportunities. Whether it's discussing household responsibilities, career decisions, or personal aspirations, resilient leaders can effectively communicate their needs and expectations, fostering stronger and more balanced relationships.

Mastering the art of negotiation is essential for resilient leaders working in male-dominated industries. Drawing on the concepts in *Don't Leave Money on the Table: Negotiation Strategies*, the L.A.T.T.E. negotiation framework offers a practical approach to advocating for success. Resilient leaders can navigate the challenges of both professional and personal negotiations by building relationships, focusing on shared interests, and asserting their worth. With these strategies, leaders can break barriers, overcome biases, and achieve favorable outcomes, paving the way for a more inclusive and equitable future.

THE ART OF NEGOTIATION: STRATEGIES FOR EFFECTIVE BUSINESS NEGOTIATIONS

Resilient leaders who aspire to achieve desirable outcomes in business negotiations must be aware of several areas within the art of negotiation. By mastering these strategies within your leadership, you can enhance effectiveness and secure mutually beneficial agreements. Here are four crucial elements for resilient leaders:

Thorough preparation is the initial step in achieving effective negotiation. Resilient leaders recognize the importance of investing time to thoroughly understand all parties' goals, interests, and constraints. In my in-person negotiation workshops, I've shared that in my experience, nearly 80%

of negotiation happens in the preparation phase. This necessitates conducting extensive research, analyzing data, and identifying potential areas of compromise. By being well-prepared, you can confidently enter negotiations with a strategic advantage that positions you favorably to achieve desired outcomes.

Effective communication is a cornerstone of successful negotiation. Resilient leaders recognize the importance of possessing strong interpersonal skills to effectively convey their ideas, actively listen to the perspectives of others, and establish rapport. When you're engaged in active listening, you not only hear what the other party is saying, but you also hear what isn't being said; thus, with more information, you can make better-informed decisions. Leaders must articulate their interests and priorities clearly and concisely. Doing so enables a deeper understanding among all parties involved and lays the foundation for mutually beneficial discussions. This communication approach fosters an open and respectful dialogue environment; resilient leaders can create a collaborative atmosphere that facilitates the identification of mutually beneficial solutions, leading to successful outcomes.

Approach negotiations with a problem-solving mindset, focusing on finding mutually beneficial solutions. Instead of fixating solely on positions or demands, strive to comprehend all parties' underlying interests and motivations by asking open-ended questions and actively listening to responses. This understanding allows you to explore innovative and creative approaches that address multiple needs and generate value for everyone. One secret to effectively overcome impasses and reach win-win outcomes is thinking outside the box and considering alternative options to reach an agreement.

For instance, imagine a negotiation between your company and a supplier over pricing terms. A resilient leader who embraces problem-solving and creativity might dig deeper to understand the supplier's motivations beyond profit margins. One might discover that the supplier values long-term relationships and reliable partnerships. With this insight, the leader could propose a pricing structure that balances profitability for both parties while ensuring a stable and enduring collaboration, thus offering a solution to a challenge that is mutually beneficial.

In another scenario, consider a negotiation between two teams within an organization regarding resource allocation. A resilient leader adept in problem-solving and creativity would seek to explore the core interests driving each team leader's requests. By identifying common ground and exploring alternative resource distribution strategies, the leaders could craft a solution that optimizes resource utilization, fosters team cooperation and aligns with the organization's overall goals.By employing problem-solving and creative thinking in negotiations, resilient leaders can transcend traditional win-lose dynamics and boost resiliency through mutually beneficial outcomes.

I'd also like to emphasize the importance of not falling into the trap of being fixed on one solution over another. Flexibility and adaptability are crucial qualities for resilient leaders in negotiations. The dynamic nature of the negotiation process often presents unexpected challenges and changing circumstances. Leaders who can adjust their strategies, explore different viewpoints, and consider concessions when necessary are more likely to achieve favorable outcomes for all parties involved. A powerful technique is to remember to be open to compromise without compromising essential requests that aid resiliency, which allows leaders to maintain progress and momentum toward their desired objectives.

Be aware that there are potential downsides to extreme flexibility and adaptability and under stressful conditions, it can become tempting to lose balance of boundaries. As a general rule of thumb, balance being open to compromise and ensuring you do not compromise on core interests or values. Being too flexible without clearly defining non-negotiables can lead to conceding on areas that would support success and could result in walking away with less-than-desirable outcomes. Focus on boosting your skills to discern and make strategic choices that align with resiliency objectives and intentionally support your values in decisions.

Remember that negotiation is a multifaceted process requiring resilient leaders to master several key steps and areas. By adequately preparing, effectively communicating, employing problem-solving techniques, and remaining flexible, leaders can enhance their negotiation skills and achieve desired outcomes in business negotiations.

SELF-ADVOCACY IN NEGOTIATIONS: NAVIGATING PERSONAL AND PROFESSIONAL GOALS

As emphasized throughout this book, self-awareness is crucial for resilient leaders. This extends to recognizing the value of knowing your worth, and strongly understanding one's skills and accomplishments. Self-efficacy is the antidote to doubt and even imposter syndrome, which could arise when one is negotiating. You're able to achieve both personal and professional goals with greater resilience when you're unapologetic in your approach to being your own best advocate.

Setting clear goals is another essential aspect. By defining personal and professional objectives, leaders establish specific and measurable targets that guide their negotiation strategy. This allows them to stay focused and pursue outcomes aligned with their aspirations. For instance, a resilient leader in a male-dominated field might set a goal of achieving a leadership position within a certain timeframe, driving their negotiation efforts towards opportunities that enable career growth.

Thorough research and preparation are key to negotiation success. Leaders should delve into the negotiation context, understanding industry standards, market trends, and competitor insights. By preparing compelling arguments backed by data, they strengthen their positions. For example, a resilient leader aiming for a promotion in a male-dominated industry might gather evidence of their exceptional performance and contributions to demonstrate their readiness for advancement.

Understanding the other party is crucial in finding common ground and building mutually beneficial solutions. Leaders should put themselves in the other party's shoes, considering their interests, motivations, and potential objections. This empathetic approach fosters constructive dialogue and increases the likelihood of reaching agreements that satisfy both sides. For instance, a resilient leader negotiating a partnership with a male-dominated company can seek to understand their priorities and tailor their proposal accordingly, demonstrating a win-win scenario.

Effective communication skills are vital for self-advocacy. Leaders should clearly articulate their ideas, needs, and expectations while actively listening to others. This fosters open and respectful dialogue, promoting understanding and cooperation. For example, a resilient leader working in a male-dominated industry can effectively communicate their vision for a project, actively engaging with stakeholders and incorporating their input to build consensus.

Assertiveness and confidence play a significant role in negotiation outcomes. Leaders should express their goals and boundaries assertively while maintaining professionalism. Confidence in their abilities and worth enhances their negotiation position and establishes credibility. For instance, a resilient leader advocating for a promotion can confidently present their qualifications and make a compelling case for advancement.

Developing a support network is essential for resilience. Leaders should surround themselves with mentors, sponsors, and peers who provide guidance and support. Collaborating with others who understand the unique challenges of a male-dominated industry can offer valuable insights and strengthen negotiation efforts. For example, a resilient leader may seek guidance from a mentor who has successfully navigated negotiations in a similar industry, leveraging their experience and expertise.

Flexibility and adaptability are key when encountering unexpected circumstances. Leaders should be open to considering alternative solutions and adjusting their negotiation strategies accordingly. This adaptability increases their chances of achieving the best possible outcome. For instance, a resilient leader facing a sudden change in market conditions may pivot their negotiation approach, exploring new avenues and opportunities to maintain progress toward their goals.

Understanding different negotiation styles is crucial for effective self-advocacy. Leaders should adapt their approach based on the specific context and goals. Whether it's a collaborative or competitive style, choosing the appropriate style aligns with their objectives. For example, a resilient leader in a male-dominated industry may employ a collaborative negotiation style to foster cooperation and build long-term relationships, ensuring a more inclusive and supportive environment.

Lastly, leaders must address gender biases that may impact the negotiation process. They can overcome these obstacles by challenging stereotypes and biases and emphasizing their expertise, achievements, and the value they bring to the table. For instance, resilient leaders can proactively address biased assumptions by presenting concrete evidence of their capabilities and highlighting the positive impact they have made in their role.

Resilient leaders in male-dominated industries can effectively navigate challenges and complexities by proactively focusing on these ten areas of self-advocacy in negotiations. Through effective self-advocacy, they can maximize their potential, achieve personal and professional goals, and contribute to creating a more equitable and inclusive business environment.

Resilient Leader Profile: Shellye Archambeau

Shellye Archambeau is a business pioneer, renowned technology executive, and author of *Unapologetically Ambitious: Take Risks, Break Barriers, and Create Success on Your Own Terms*. Throughout her career, Archambeau has exhibited exceptional negotiation skills in her professional journey and personal life decisions. Since her book was released it has been a personal favorite and I've gifted it to many of the Resilient Leader Alumni.

Archambeau shares her experiences as a Black woman navigating the predominantly male-dominated tech industry. She emphasizes the importance of negotiating for oneself and taking risks to achieve success. Archambeau's negotiations encompassed various aspects of her career, such as salary negotiations, promotions, and opportunities for advancement.

One notable example of Archambeau's negotiation prowess is her role as the CEO of MetricStream, a governance, risk management, and compliance software company. She successfully led the company through a vital negotiation phase, securing major partnerships with industry giants during her tenure. Archambeau's strategic negotiation skills played a significant role in establishing these partnerships, which led to substantial business growth and cemented MetricStream's position in the market.

Beyond the corporate realm, Archambeau's negotiations extended to her personal life decisions. Her book recounts instances where she negotiated the delicate balance between her career and her family life. Archambeau made intentional decisions to prioritize her family's well-being while still pursuing her ambitions, demonstrating her ability to negotiate and find solutions that aligned with her values and goals.

Archambeau's negotiations inspire me and other leaders, particularly those facing similar challenges in male-dominated industries. Through her determination, resilience, and negotiation skills, she broke barriers and created her path to success. Archambeau's story encourages individuals to advocate for themselves, take calculated risks, and negotiate assertively to achieve their goals and dreams.

Shellye Archambeau's career and life decisions exemplify the traits of a resilient leader. Her ability to navigate negotiations, whether in professional collaborations or personal choices, demonstrates her strategic mindset, tenacity, and commitment to pursuing success on her terms. Archambeau's experiences and insights serve as an empowering guide for individuals seeking to break barriers, embrace ambition, and negotiate effectively to create their path to success. I also recommend following Shellye on LinkedIn. Her strategies are profoundly relevant for navigating challenges.

WIN-WIN SOLUTIONS: CONFLICT NAVIGATIONS

Resilient leaders strive to adapt win-win solutions and conflict navigation strategies in the workplace as a tool to avoid burnout while embracing resiliency. I think I can safely assume that, having chosen this book to read, you will agree that win-win solutions promote a collaborative work environment. By focusing on creating mutually beneficial outcomes, leaders can encourage teamwork, enhance employee satisfaction, and build stronger relationships among team members. Win-win solutions also contribute to improved productivity and innovation as individuals feel valued and motivated to contribute their best efforts when they perceive their interests are being considered.

Also, win-win solutions help maintain long-term relationships with clients, customers, and stakeholders. By prioritizing the satisfaction and success of all parties involved, resilient leaders can establish a reputation for fairness, reliability, and trustworthiness. This can lead to repeat business, referrals, and positive word-of-mouth, benefiting the organization's growth and sustainability.

However, adopting win-win solutions and conflict navigation strategies has potential downsides or cons. One challenge is that reaching a win-win outcome often requires more time and effort than simply imposing a decision or accepting a compromise. The process may involve active listening, extensive communication, and finding creative alternatives that satisfy multiple interests. This can be demanding and may require patience and persistence on the part of the leader.

Another potential drawback is that not all individuals or parties may be receptive to a win-win approach. In highly competitive environments or when individuals prioritize personal gain over collective success, achieving consensus or cooperation may be challenging. Some individuals may resist collaboration and instead focus solely on achieving their goals. In such cases, the leader may need to carefully navigate and address these conflicts to find a mutually beneficial solution.

While adopting win-win solutions and conflict navigation strategies offer numerous advantages, including fostering collaboration, maintaining relationships, and promoting innovation, resilient leaders must be aware of the potential cons. These may include the need for additional time and effort and challenges in navigating conflicts with individuals who prioritize personal gain. By understanding these potential drawbacks, leaders can proactively address them and maximize the benefits of win-win approaches in the workplace.

Conflict Management

The L.A.T.T.E. method is helpful for conflict management, particularly for underrepresented leaders in male-dominated industries. Here is how you can use each step of the method in conflict management:

Look at the details: In conflicts, it is essential to consider all the details of the situation, including any power dynamics or biases at play. As an underrepresented leader in a male-dominated industry, you may need to pay extra attention to issues related to gender or other identities. Look at the details of the situation and consider all the factors contributing to the conflict.

Anticipate the challenges: Once you clearly understand the details of the situation, anticipate the challenges you may face when trying to resolve the conflict. For example, if the conflict involves someone dismissing your ideas or expertise because of your identity, anticipate they may resist your perspective. Anticipating these challenges can help you prepare for them and develop strategies for addressing them.

Think about the walk-away point: Before engaging in a conflict, it is crucial to consider your walk-away point - the point at which you are no longer willing to continue negotiating or compromising. As an underrepresented leader, you may need to be particularly aware of this, as you may face more pressure to compromise or give in. Consider what you are willing to accept and what you are not, and be prepared to walk away if necessary.

Talk it through. Once you have prepared yourself, it is time to engage in the conflict directly. Talk it through with the other party, being mindful of the details and challenges you have identified. Use active listening skills to understand the other person's perspective and communicate your perspective clearly and respectfully. Be open to finding mutually beneficial solutions.

Evaluate the options. Finally, evaluate the options that emerge from the conflict. Consider how well they address the underlying issues and power dynamics and whether they represent a fair and equitable solution. If necessary, be willing to seek out additional resources or support to help you evaluate the options.

The L.A.T.T.E. method can be a valuable tool for underrepresented leaders in male-dominated industries to navigate conflicts confidently and clearly. You can approach conflict management strategically and effectively by looking at the details, anticipating challenges, thinking about the walk-away point, talking it through, and evaluating the options.

Team Building

The L.A.T.T.E. method can be used as a team-building cycle, where each step is applied iteratively to strengthen team dynamics and resolve conflicts. Here is how each step of the method can be used in team building:

Look at the details: Start by looking at the details of the team dynamics, including each member's strengths, weaknesses, and communication styles. Consider any power dynamics or biases at play, and identify any sources of tension or conflict within the team.

Anticipate the challenges: Once you understand the team dynamics, anticipate your challenges in building a cohesive and collaborative team. For example, if there are personality conflicts or differences in communication styles, anticipate that these may lead to misunderstandings or tension. Anticipating these challenges can help you prepare for them and develop strategies for addressing them.

Think about the walk-away point: Before engaging in team-building activities, consider where to step back and reassess your approach. This could include situations where team members are unwilling to engage in constructive dialogue or significant resistance to change. Identify what you are willing to accept and not, and be prepared to adjust your approach if necessary.

Talk it through: Engage the team in dialogue and active listening exercises to build understanding and collaboration. Encourage team members to share their perspectives and actively listen to one another. Create a safe and inclusive environment where everyone feels comfortable contributing.

Evaluate the options: After engaging in dialogue, evaluate the options for building a more cohesive and collaborative team. Consider strategies for addressing any conflicts or sources of tension, and identify opportunities for building on the team's strengths. Be open to feedback and input from team members, and work collaboratively to develop a plan for moving forward.

Applying the L.A.T.T.E. method iteratively can create a cycle of continuous improvement and team building that strengthens team dynamics, resolves conflicts and promotes collaboration and inclusivity.

Chapter 11

TEAM BUILDING CONFLICT MANAGEMENT: NAVIGATING DIFFERENCES FOR COLLABORATION

Dear Resilient Leaders,

I hope this email finds you well, leading your teams through challenges and inspiring collaboration. Today, I would like to discuss an important aspect of team dynamics: conflict management.

As leaders, we understand that conflicts and disagreements are inevitable within any team. The outcome of these conflicts is ultimately determined by how we approach them. By embracing conflict as an opportunity for growth and learning, we can harness its potential to strengthen relationships and enhance team performance.

When conflicts arise, it is important to create a safe space for open and honest communication. Encourage team members to express their concerns and perspectives without fear of judgment or retaliation. Active listening plays a crucial role in this process. By attentively hearing and understanding each individual's point of view, we can foster mutual respect and build trust within the team.

Empathy is another vital skill in conflict management. Recognizing and acknowledging the emotions and perspectives of others helps us develop a deeper understanding of their positions. It allows us to approach conflicts with compassion, seeking resolutions that accommodate various viewpoints and balance individual needs with collective goals.

Effective conflict management also requires focusing on common goals. By reminding team members of the shared objectives they are working towards, we can redirect their energy from personal conflicts to collaborative problem-solving. This shift in focus encourages creativity, cooperation, and a commitment to finding win-win solutions.

Furthermore, as leaders, it is crucial to lead by example. Model respectful and constructive behavior in your interactions with team members. Show appreciation for diverse perspectives and encourage a culture of open-mindedness and inclusivity. By setting the tone for constructive conflict management, you empower your team to engage in productive discussions and find resolutions that benefit everyone involved.

I encourage you to reflect on your team's conflict management practices and consider areas for improvement. Foster a culture that embraces differences, encourages open dialogue, and values the collective strength of the team. By nurturing a collaborative and supportive work environment, you will empower your team to thrive and achieve exceptional results.

I wish you continued success in your leadership journey, marked by effective conflict management and collaborative team building.

Best,

Jacqueline V. Twillie
Founder of ZeroGap.co
Creator of the Resilient Leaders Program

Resilient leaders in male-dominated industries recognize the importance of considering four key areas in their leadership strategy: team building, conflict management, navigating differences, and fostering collaboration. These areas are essential for creating an inclusive and supportive work environment that empowers individuals and maximizes their potential. Let's delve deeper into each area, providing examples to illustrate their significance.

Firstly, team building is crucial for resilient leaders. They actively seek to build diverse and inclusive teams, fostering an environment where individuals from different backgrounds, genders, and perspectives can thrive. Resilient leaders cultivate a sense of belonging and psychological safety, encouraging open communication, trust, and collaboration among team members. For instance, they may organize team-building activities that promote mutual understanding and appreciation, such as diversity training workshops or mentorship programs that pair employees from different backgrounds.

Secondly, conflict management is a skill that resilient leaders excel at. They understand that conflicts can arise within teams and male-dominated industries due to differences in opinions, communication styles, and work approaches. Resilient leaders manage conflicts constructively and respectfully, ensuring they do not escalate or create a hostile work environment. They encourage open dialogue among team members, actively listen to differing viewpoints, and mediate discussions to find common ground. Leaders can leverage diverse perspectives to drive innovation and improve decision-making processes by promoting healthy conflict resolution.

Thirdly, resilient leaders in male-dominated industries navigate differences effectively. They acknowledge and value the unique strengths and perspectives that individuals bring to the table. These leaders proactively address biases and stereotypes in their industries, ensuring everyone's contributions are recognized and valued equally. They foster an inclusive culture by encouraging individuals to share their experiences, ideas, and concerns without fear of judgment or marginalization. For example, they may implement diversity and inclusion training programs that raise awareness of unconscious biases and provide tools to challenge them, thus fostering a more equitable and inclusive workplace.

Lastly, collaboration is essential for resilient leaders. They understand that success in male-dominated industries relies on effective collaboration. Resilient leaders create opportunities for collaboration within and outside their organizations to leverage diverse perspectives and expertise. They establish networks and partnerships with other organizations, industry associations, and community groups to promote knowledge-sharing and mentorship opportunities. By encouraging collaboration, leaders empower individuals to learn from each other, broaden their skill sets, and collectively overcome challenges.

Resilient leaders in male-dominated industries prioritize team building, conflict management, navigating differences, and fostering collaboration. By implementing strategies that promote inclusivity, open communication, and respect, these leaders create a supportive work environment that encourages the full potential of every individual. Ultimately, such leadership approaches contribute to the success and resilience of the leaders and their organizations in male-dominated industries.

Resilient Leader Profile: Clarence Avant

The late Clarence Avant, a prominent music executive and entrepreneur, exemplified the qualities of a resilient leader. Known as the "Godfather of Black Music," Avant's remarkable career was defined by his ability to navigate complex negotiations and advocate for the interests of multiple parties. One notable example of his impactful role as a negotiator was his involvement in securing the Michael Jackson soundtrack for the movie *E.T. the Extra-Terrestrial*.

During the early 1980s, when the iconic film *E.T. the Extra-Terrestrial* was being produced, its director Steven Spielberg desired to incorporate a song by Michael Jackson into the soundtrack. However, negotiations with Jackson's record label, Epic Records, proved challenging. Avant, recognizing the potential synergies and immense value of such a collaboration, stepped in to bridge the gap between the parties involved.

Avant's resilience and expertise in the music industry allowed him to understand the motivations and interests of all parties. He leveraged his network and influence to foster dialogue and find common ground. By utilizing his negotiation skills and industry knowledge, Avant facilitated a mutually beneficial agreement. Ultimately, a deal was struck, including Michael Jackson's chart-topping hit "Someone in the Dark" in the film's soundtrack. This collaboration not only enhanced the artistic value of the movie but also became a significant commercial success, solidifying Jackson's position as a global superstar.

Avant's role in negotiating for all parties to secure the Michael Jackson soundtrack for *E.T. the Extra-Terrestrial* showcases his leadership resilience. His legacy exemplifies the ability to navigate complex situations, understand diverse perspectives, and find creative solutions that benefit multiple stakeholders. Avant's capacity to build relationships, advocate for artists, and drive successful outcomes has earned him respect and admiration within the music industry.

Throughout his career, Clarence Avant consistently demonstrated the qualities of a resilient leader. His ability to navigate challenging negotiations and bridge gaps between parties contributed to his success and shaped the trajectory of the music industry as a whole. Avant's story inspires us, reminding us of the importance of resilience, adaptability, and collaboration in achieving remarkable outcomes in adversity.

BUILDING HABITS: TRUST, COMMUNICATION, CONFLICT, AND COLLABORATION

Conflict is an inherent part of human interaction, and in the realm of leadership, it often arises due to diverse perspectives, competing interests, or differing objectives. However, resilient leaders possess a unique ability to transform conflict into an opportunity for growth, collaboration, and increased agency. By building healthy habits that foster trust, communication with diverse individuals, and converting conflict into collaboration, these leaders empower their teams to overcome challenges and achieve remarkable outcomes. Nevertheless, recognizing the importance of psychological safety is crucial, as there are times when walking away from an unsafe conflict situation becomes necessary for the overall well-being of the individuals involved. In this section, we explore the power of resilient leadership in leveraging conflict to drive positive change while advocating for psychological safety.

Resilient leaders understand that building healthy habits is foundational to handling conflict effectively. By cultivating an environment that encourages trust, they establish a strong foundation upon which individuals can express their ideas, concerns, and perspectives without fear of judgment or retribution. Trust is nurtured through consistent and transparent communication, active listening, and demonstrating empathy. By actively practicing these habits, leaders foster an environment where conflict is seen as an opportunity for growth rather than a threat to harmony.

Effective communication lies at the heart of resolving conflicts and harnessing their potential. Resilient leaders recognize the value of diverse life experiences and perspectives and actively seek opportunities to engage with individuals from different backgrounds. By embracing diversity, these leaders create an inclusive space that allows for various ideas and opinions to be expressed. By listening attentively and valuing every voice, resilient leaders promote open dialogue and collaborative problem-solving, leading to innovative and inclusive solutions.

Rather than avoiding or suppressing conflict, resilient leaders understand the transformative power it holds. They view conflict as an opportunity to break down barriers, challenge assumptions, and create new pathways for growth. By reframing conflict as a natural part of the decision-making process, these leaders encourage their teams to approach disagreements with curiosity, respect, and a focus on finding common ground. Through effective facilitation and mediation, they guide the conflicting parties towards a collaborative mindset, fostering a sense of shared ownership and the collective pursuit of a common goal.

While resilient leaders understand the potential for growth within the conflict, they also recognize the importance of psychological safety. In situations where conflicts become toxic, destructive, or threaten the well-being of individuals involved, it is crucial for leaders to intervene and assess the level of psychological safety within the team. If psychological safety cannot be ensured, walking away from the conflict becomes a necessary step to protect the individuals' mental health and preserve a healthy work environment. Resilient leaders prioritize the well-being of their team members and actively work towards establishing an environment where everyone feels safe, respected, and heard.

Conflict, when managed effectively, can serve as a catalyst for growth and collaboration within organizations. Resilient leaders harness the power of conflict by building healthy habits that foster trust, promoting communication with diverse perspectives, and transforming conflicts into opportunities for collaboration. However, these leaders also recognize the importance of psychological safety and know when to walk away from unhealthy conflict situations. By embracing conflict as a natural part of the leadership journey, resilient leaders enable their teams to flourish, achieve remarkable results, and create a culture of continuous improvement and innovation.

Jacqueline V. Twillie

RESILIENT CONFLICT NAVIGATION CIRCLE: TURNING DIFFERENCES INTO OPPORTUNITIES

The Resilient Conflict Navigation Circle is a comprehensive framework designed to guide leaders in managing conflict and transforming differences into opportunities for growth. It consists of eight interconnected areas represented by individual circles, each addressing a specific aspect of conflict resolution and collaboration. This powerful tool empowers leaders to navigate conflicts with confidence and effectiveness, promoting a culture of resilience, open communication, and shared understanding within their teams.

Self-Awareness: The first circle of the wheel emphasizes the importance of self-awareness in conflict management. Resilient leaders recognize their own triggers, biases, and communication styles, enabling them to approach conflicts with objectivity and empathy.

Active Listening: Effective communication lies at the heart of conflict resolution. The second circle emphasizes the skill of active listening, encouraging leaders to attentively engage with all parties involved, and understanding their perspectives, needs, and underlying concerns.

Emotional Intelligence: Emotional intelligence plays a pivotal role in conflict management. This circle highlights the significance of understanding and regulating emotions during conflicts, fostering an atmosphere of empathy, respect, and constructive dialogue.

Collaboration: Collaboration is the key to transforming conflicts into opportunities for growth. This circle focuses on cultivating a mindset of collaboration, encouraging leaders to foster an environment where all parties work together to find creative solutions and common ground.

Mediation and Facilitation: Conflict resolution often requires a neutral third party to facilitate productive conversations. This circle emphasizes the skills of mediation and facilitation, equipping leaders with techniques to guide conflicting parties toward understanding, compromise, and mutually beneficial outcomes.

Cultural Competence: In today's diverse workplaces, conflicts can arise due to cultural differences. This circle highlights the importance of cultural competence, enabling leaders to navigate conflicts sensitively and respectfully while promoting inclusivity and understanding across diverse backgrounds.

Problem-Solving: Effective conflict resolution involves addressing underlying issues and finding sustainable solutions. This circle emphasizes the skill of problem-solving, encouraging leaders to adopt a proactive approach to identify and address the root causes of conflicts.

Learning and Growth: The final circle of the wheel underscores the importance of continuous learning and growth. Resilient leaders recognize that conflicts provide valuable learning opportunities for individuals and teams. They encourage reflection, feedback, and a growth mindset, enabling everyone involved to develop and thrive through the resolution process.

The Resilient Conflict Navigation Circle provides a comprehensive roadmap for leaders to manage conflicts effectively, turning differences into opportunities for growth, collaboration, and innovation. By utilizing this framework, leaders can foster a culture of resilience, trust, and open communication, ultimately driving positive change within their organizations.

WHAT'S YOUR STORY: HARNESSING THE STRENGTH OF DIFFERENT PERSPECTIVES

"What's Your Story?" is a leadership activity designed to foster understanding, empathy, and collaboration among team members by exploring and appreciating their diverse backgrounds, experiences, and perspectives. This activity encourages participants to share their personal stories, allowing them to gain insights into each other's unique journeys and viewpoints. By harnessing the strength of different perspectives, resilient leaders create an inclusive environment that values diversity and promotes teamwork.

Materials Needed:

- A comfortable and private space for the activity
- Flipcharts or whiteboards
- Markers
- Note cards or sticky notes

- Timer

Instructions:

Begin by setting the stage. Gather the participants in a comfortable and private space.

Introduce the activity by explaining the importance of understanding and appreciating diverse perspectives in a team. Emphasize that this activity aims to create a safe and non-judgmental environment where everyone's stories are respected. Then, explain the activity. Explain that each participant will have a designated time to share their personal story. Emphasize that the focus should be on experiences, values, and events that have shaped their perspectives rather than personal details that may make individuals uncomfortable sharing.

Encourage participants to be authentic, open, and respectful when sharing their stories.

Next, define time slots. Divide the total activity time by the number of participants to determine the time each person will have to share their story. For larger groups, consider having shorter time slots to ensure everyone gets an opportunity to speak.

Once the activity has been explained and organized, you can activate the storytelling session. Begin the storytelling session by selecting a participant to share their story. Set a timer for the allotted time and remind participants to respect the time limit. Encourage active listening and remind participants to avoid interrupting or passing judgment during the storytelling process. Participants can take notes on key points or questions that arise during each person's story.

Afterward, pause for reflection and engage in discussion. After each participant has shared their story, facilitate a reflective discussion to explore commonalities, differences, and themes that emerged. Use flipcharts or whiteboards to capture key insights, connections, and observations. Encourage participants to ask clarifying questions or share their thoughts on the stories they heard.

As a bonus step, identify strengths and opportunities. Lead a discussion to identify the strengths, perspectives, and talents that emerged from the activity. Encourage participants to consider how these diverse perspectives can be harnessed to drive innovation, problem-solving, and collaboration within the team or organization. Explore opportunities for leveraging these strengths in future projects or initiatives.

To maximize the impact of this activity, take time to summarize the main takeaways and key learnings from the activity. Discuss ways to promote ongoing understanding and appreciation of diverse perspectives in day-to-day interactions. Encourage participants to continue building connections and seeking opportunities to learn from each other's experiences beyond this activity.

The "What's Your Story?" activity serves as a powerful tool for resilient leaders to harness the strength of different perspectives within their teams. By creating an inclusive space for personal storytelling, leaders foster empathy, understanding, and collaboration. This activity enables participants to appreciate the rich diversity within the team and provides a foundation for leveraging those diverse perspectives to drive innovation, problem-solving, and teamwork. By embracing the power of storytelling, resilient leaders empower their teams to thrive in a dynamic and inclusive environment.

Chapter 12

STRATEGIC NETWORKING & PARTNERSHIPS: CREATING CONNECTIONS FOR SUCCESS

Dear Resilient Leader,

I hope this email finds you in good health and high spirits. As a fellow advocate for strategic networking and partnerships, I wanted to take this opportunity to discuss a vital aspect of building professional relationships: maintaining mutually beneficial connections.

In today's interconnected world, it is important to nurture a personal board of directors, consisting of individuals from various professional backgrounds who provide guidance, support, and valuable insights as you navigate your career. Just as a successful organization thrives with a strong board of directors, so too can individuals benefit from cultivating a similar network of trusted advisors and partners.

With that said, it's crucial to remember that these relationships should be nurtured and maintained in a way that is mutually beneficial. While it's natural to seek guidance and assistance from our network, it is equally important to contribute and offer support whenever possible. A truly successful relationship is built on a foundation of reciprocity.

To ensure you maintain these mutually beneficial relationships, here are a few key considerations:

Offer support and assistance: *Actively seek opportunities to assist your connections by sharing relevant resources, introducing them to potential partners, or providing advice based on your expertise. By doing so, you reinforce the trust and goodwill within your network.*

Show genuine interest: *Take the time to understand the goals, challenges, and aspirations of your connections. Regularly engage in meaningful conversations, actively listen, and provide support and encouragement where needed. This demonstrates your commitment to their success and strengthens the bond between you.*

Recognize and acknowledge: *When your connections provide valuable insights, guidance, or assistance, it's important to express your gratitude. Acknowledge their contributions, whether through a heartfelt thank-you message, a small token of appreciation, or by highlighting their achievements in your professional network. Recognition reinforces the importance of their role in your success.*

Give without expectation: *Sometimes, the most valuable contributions we make to our connections are driven solely by our desire to see them thrive. Offer your expertise, time, or resources without expecting an immediate return. This selfless approach fosters a culture of reciprocity and ultimately leads to stronger, long-lasting relationships.*

By nurturing and maintaining your personal board of directors with these principles in mind, you will create a supportive network that propels your success and that of those around you. Remember, the true power of networking lies not only in what we gain but also in what we give.

I hope you find these insights valuable as you continue to forge meaningful connections and create partnerships that will drive your professional growth. If you have any thoughts or experiences you'd like to share on this topic, I would be delighted to hear from you.

I wish you continued success in all your endeavors.

Warm regards,

Jacqueline V. Twillie
Founder of ZeroGap.co
Creator of the Resilient Leaders Program

Jacqueline V. Twillie

THE HARMONY OF STRATEGIC NETWORKING: BUILDING RELATIONSHIPS UPON RESONANCE

In our interconnected world, strategic networking has emerged as a crucial aspect of professional success. It involves building meaningful relationships, forging partnerships, and leveraging collective strengths. While networking is often associated with expanding one's contact list, true effectiveness lies in the harmony created through resonant connections. In this section, we explore the concept of resonance in networking and highlight its importance in contrast to dissonance.

Resonance in networking refers to individuals aligning their values, goals, and interests to create mutually beneficial relationships. When there is resonance, the interaction becomes natural, effortless, and synergistic. It goes beyond superficial connections, creating a deep sense of understanding and shared purpose. Resonance enables individuals to tap into each other's strengths, support one another, and propel their professional growth together.

Resonance is of utmost importance in networking, surpassing the significance of dissonance. Resonant connections foster genuine relationships, collaborative opportunities, and emotional support, enabling individuals to achieve growth and success together. Embracing resonance in networking enhances authenticity, alignment, and mutual understanding, leading to more meaningful and fruitful professional connections.

Resonance cultivates deep connections, fostering trust and authenticity for stronger relationships. It promotes collaboration by aligning expertise, resources, and goals, encouraging support and knowledge-sharing. Conversely, dissonance creates superficial interactions and hinders collaboration due to conflicting interests and values.

Resonant relationships offer emotional support, providing guidance, motivation, and empathy. They invest in each other's success and well-being, while dissonant relationships can lead to isolation and a lack of support. Resonant connections also open doors to growth opportunities, expanding horizons and accessing new networks, fostering innovation. In contrast, dissonance restricts progress by creating barriers arising from conflicting interests and values.

When cultivating deep connections, seek to understand your values, goals, and aspirations clearly. This self-awareness enables the identification of individuals who align with your professional journey. Actively listen to others, seek to comprehend their perspectives, and demonstrate empathy. By doing so, resonant qualities can be recognized, leading to genuine connections based on shared understanding. Look for individuals who share similar values and goals, engage in conversations that uncover commonalities, and explore opportunities for mutual support. Dedicate time and effort to nurture these relationships, engaging in meaningful conversations, offering support, and celebrating achievements. Show sincere interest in their growth and well-being.

The harmony of strategic networking lies in building relationships upon resonance. Deep connections, characterized by shared values, goals, and interests, bring authenticity, collaboration, emotional support, and growth opportunities. By cultivating resonant connections and embracing the power of resonance, individuals can forge deep and meaningful relationships that propel their professional success in ways that dissonance cannot achieve. So, let us seek harmony in our networking efforts, fostering deep connections that bring us closer to our goals.

CULTIVATING UNLIKELY PARTNERSHIPS: LEVERAGING COLLECTIVE STRENGTHS

In the realm of business and innovation, the concept of cultivating unlikely partnerships has gained traction in recent years. Unlikely partnerships involve joining forces with individuals or organizations that may seem unconventional or unexpected. This approach, popularized by Jack Manning Bancroft, founder of AIME and author of *Hoodie Economics*, has demonstrated the power of leveraging collective strengths to drive transformative change. This section explores the value of cultivating unlikely partnerships and how they can lead to remarkable outcomes.

Unlikely partnerships have the remarkable ability to unleash creativity and foster innovation. These partnerships create a fertile ground for fresh ideas and unique problem-solving approaches by bringing together diverse perspectives, expertise, and backgrounds. When individuals or organizations collaborate outside their traditional circles, they can tap into unexplored avenues, challenge assumptions, and break free from conventional thinking. This dynamic interplay of different strengths and perspectives often results in groundbreaking innovations and game-changing solutions.

Cultivating unlikely partnerships enables individuals and organizations to expand their networks and access additional resources. When individuals come together from different industries, disciplines, or backgrounds, they bring their networks and resources. This broadens the reach and capabilities of the partnership, unlocking new opportunities, connections, and avenues for growth. By leveraging collective strengths, unlikely partnerships can tap into diverse skills, experiences, and knowledge, creating a powerful synergy that amplifies their impact.

Unlikely partnerships have shown tremendous potential in driving social impact and instigating positive change. When individuals or organizations with different missions or areas of expertise collaborate, they can tackle complex social issues from multiple angles. Unlikely partnerships break down silos and foster cross-sector collaboration, enabling the pooling of resources, knowledge, and influence. This collective effort towards a common goal amplifies the potential for transformative change, addressing societal challenges in innovative and holistic ways.

Cultivating unlikely partnerships is not without its challenges. Differences in organizational culture, communication styles, or objectives may arise. However, these challenges can be transformed into opportunities for growth and learning. Unlikely partnerships require open-mindedness, effective communication, and a willingness to embrace diverse perspectives. As individuals or organizations navigate these challenges, they build resilience, adaptability, and an expanded capacity to collaborate across boundaries.

Cultivating unlikely partnerships is a powerful approach that can fuel creativity, expand networks, and drive meaningful change. Individuals and organizations can leverage collective strengths and unleash their full potential by breaking free from traditional boundaries and embracing diverse collaborations. Inspired by the concept popularized by Jack Manning Bancroft in "Hoodie Economics," these partnerships can disrupt industries, foster innovation, and make a lasting impact on society. So, let us embrace the possibilities of unlikely partnerships and harness their collective strength to create a brighter and more prosperous future.

STRATEGIC NETWORKING & PARTNERSHIPS

In male-dominated industries where underrepresented leaders are trying to establish themselves, building a strong network can be essential to building resilience. Networking provides access to resources, mentorship, and support, which can be vital for navigating challenges and overcoming obstacles in these industries.

Networking can take many forms, from attending industry events and conferences to connecting with colleagues on social media or through professional organizations. By building a network of like-minded individuals, underrepresented leaders can access information and opportunities they might not otherwise have and establish relationships with mentors who can offer guidance and support.

Networking can also help underrepresented leaders develop the skills they need to succeed in male-dominated industries. Through networking, they can learn from others who have faced similar challenges and gain insights into the expectations and norms of the industry. This can help them navigate potential biases or stereotypes and develop the confidence and resilience necessary to succeed.

Additionally, networking can help underrepresented leaders build their visibility and influence within their industry. By attending events and engaging with others in the industry, they can develop a reputation as a thought leader and advocate for diversity and inclusion. This can help them establish themselves as a valuable contributor to the industry and gain the recognition and opportunities they deserve.

Networking is a vital tool for underrepresented leaders in male-dominated industries. By building a strong network, they can access resources and mentorship, develop the skills they need to succeed, and build their visibility and influence within their industry. By leveraging these benefits, they can build resilience and succeed despite challenges.

Personal Board of Directors

In a male-dominated industry, networking can be a powerful tool for building resilience and success as an underrepresented leader. Building strong relationships with industry members can help you gain valuable insights, resources, and support to help you navigate your unique challenges.

Networking can take many forms, from attending industry events and conferences to joining professional organizations and online communities.

It's important to intentionally build your network and seek opportunities to connect with others who share your goals and values.

One key benefit of networking is access to mentors and role models who can provide guidance and support as you advance in your career. Seek out individuals who have succeeded in the industry, be bold, and ask for their advice and insight. Many people are willing to help those just starting and can offer valuable perspectives on navigating the unique challenges of being an underrepresented leader.

Networking can also provide opportunities for collaboration and partnership. By building relationships with others in the industry, you may discover new ways to work together to achieve common goals. This can be especially valuable for underrepresented leaders who may face additional barriers to success, such as limited access to funding or resources.

Finally, networking can help you build resilience by providing a supportive community of peers who can offer encouragement and motivation when you face setbacks or challenges. By connecting with others who share your passion and commitment to the industry, you can gain the strength and resilience to overcome obstacles and achieve your goals.

Networking is key to building resilience in a male-dominated industry as an underrepresented leader. By intentionally building relationships with others in the industry, seeking mentors and role models, and collaborating with peers, you can gain valuable insights, resources, and support to help you navigate the unique challenges you may face and achieve success.

Setting up a personal board of directors can be a powerful tool for building resilience and leadership success. Your personal board of directors is a group of individuals who provide you with advice, guidance, and support as you navigate your career and personal life. Here's a guide to setting up your personal board of directors:

Step 1: Identify Your Goals and Needs.

The first step in setting up your personal board of directors is identifying your goals and needs. What are your career aspirations? What are your personal values and priorities? What are your specific challenges in your current role or industry? Once you clearly understand your goals and needs, you can identify individuals who can help you achieve them.

Step 2: Choose Your Board Members.

Choosing individuals with experience, knowledge, and connections to help you achieve your goals is important when selecting board members. Select individuals from various industries and backgrounds to ensure that you have a well-rounded perspective. Here are five examples of a personal board of director members:

- **A Mentor:** Someone who has experience in your industry and can provide guidance and advice on career advancement.
- **A Financial Advisor:** Someone who can advise on personal finance, investing, and wealth management.
- **A Marketing Expert:** Someone who can advise on building your brand, networking, and marketing yourself to potential employers or clients.
- **A Health and Wellness Coach:** Someone who can guide you on maintaining a healthy work-life balance, managing stress, and staying physically and mentally healthy.
- **A Community Leader:** Someone who is involved in your community or industry and can provide insight into trends and opportunities.

Step 3: Set Expectations

Once you have identified your board members, setting clear expectations for how you will work together is important. You should schedule regular meetings or check-ins and establish clear boundaries around confidentiality and communication.

Step 4: Nurture Your Relationships

Building and maintaining strong relationships with your board of directors is vital to its success. Communicate regularly with your board members, provide updates on your progress, and express your appreciation for their support and guidance.

Establishing a personal board of directors is a powerful tool for building resilience and success as a leader. By identifying your goals and needs, choosing the right board members, setting clear expectations, and nurturing your relationships, you can gain valuable insights, resources, and support to help you achieve your goals.

As a resilient leader, having a strong support system and professional network is crucial to help you navigate challenges and achieve your goals. Networking supports your well-being and helps you sharpen your professional skills and increase your impact. Here's a five-step plan to build your personal board of directors:

Step 1: Define Your Values and Goals

Before you start building your personal board of directors, it's essential to clarify your values and goals. Think about what you want to achieve in your personal and professional life, and what kind of people can help you get there. Consider what skills and experiences you lack and what type of support you need.

Step 2: Identify Potential Members

Once you have a clear idea of your values and goals, start identifying potential members for your personal board of directors. Look for people who share your values and have achieved success in your field or related industries. Consider seeking people who differ from you in terms of expertise, experience, and perspectives.

Step 3: Create a Connection Plan

Develop a plan to connect with potential members. Consider contacting them via LinkedIn, email, or attending industry events where they speak or attend. Research their work and accomplishments and use that knowledge to build a genuine connection.

Step 4: Consider the 4 Core Archetypes of a Personal Board of Directors.

When building your personal board of directors, consider including members who represent the following archetypes:

- **The Straight Shooter:** Someone who is honest, direct, and not afraid to challenge your thinking.
- **The Encourager:** Someone who can provide emotional support and motivation when needed.
- **The Connector:** Someone who can introduce you to new people, ideas, and opportunities.
- **The Industry Expert:** Someone with deep knowledge and experience in your field or related industries.

Step 5: Cultivate Strong Relationships

Finally, cultivate strong relationships with your personal board of directors. Connect with them regularly and share updates on your progress and challenges. Be willing to offer support and advice in return, and be open to feedback and constructive criticism.

COLLABORATION FOR IMPACT: CREATING SHARED VALUE THROUGH STRATEGIC ALLIANCES

Resilient leaders possess a deep understanding of the generational obstacles that come with being pioneers or lone individuals in a corporate environment, where there is often an expectation for them to conform to the prevailing culture. However, these leaders recognize the significance of staying true to themselves and their values, which is why they prioritize authenticity in their actions. In addition, they understand the immense importance of forging alliances both within and outside the organization, as this enables them to spearhead initiatives and create meaningful change.

Navigating the corporate landscape as a trailblazer can be challenging, as the first or only individual from a particular generation may face unique barriers and expectations. Resilient leaders acknowledge these hurdles, such as biases, preconceived notions, and resistance to change, that can hinder progress. Rather than succumbing to the pressure to assimilate, they remain steadfast in their authenticity, refusing to compromise their true selves for the sake of conformity.

Maintaining authenticity is crucial for resilient leaders because it allows them to stay connected to their values, beliefs, and purpose. By aligning their actions with their core principles, they inspire trust and foster an environment of genuine connection and collaboration. Their authenticity serves as a beacon for others, encouraging them to embrace their own individuality and contribute to the organization's success in unique and meaningful ways.

Furthermore, resilient leaders understand that building alliances is a strategic imperative. They actively seek out like-minded individuals within their organization who share their values and vision, forming alliances that amplify their impact. By collaborating with these internal allies, they are able to navigate organizational structures, garner support, and mobilize resources to drive initiatives forward. These alliances also provide a support network, offering guidance, feedback, and encouragement in the face of challenges.

Resilient leaders recognize the value of establishing alliances beyond the organization's boundaries. They engage with external stakeholders, such as industry peers, thought leaders, and community partners, to gain diverse perspectives and leverage collective expertise. These external alliances not only enhance their knowledge and understanding of the broader business landscape but also create opportunities for collaboration, innovation, and mutually beneficial partnerships.

Resilient leaders acknowledge the generational barriers they may face in a corporate environment that expects them to conform to the dominant culture. However, they remain committed to their authenticity and values. By building alliances both internally and externally, these leaders empower themselves to lead initiatives and drive meaningful impact. Their ability to stay true to themselves while forging connections with others enables them to navigate challenges, inspire their teams, and create positive change in their organizations and beyond.

Resilient Leader Profile: Jack Manning Bancroft

In the world of systems design and transformative education, Jack Manning Bancroft stands as a shining example of a resilient leader. With his unwavering dedication, innovative thinking, and commitment to social change, Bancroft has made a significant impact on the lives of countless individuals. As the founder of AIME (Australian Indigenous Mentoring Experience) and the author of *Hoodie Economics*, he has become a catalyst for positive change and an inspiration to leaders worldwide.

I've had a front-row seat to his leadership as co-CEO of AIME with my tenure starting in 2022. I speak from personal experience of his commitment to leading with values and conviction for a fairer world for us all. Jack Manning Bancroft's leadership is characterized by his visionary thinking and unwavering commitment to social impact. Recognizing the educational disparities faced by Indigenous youth in Australia, Bancroft founded AIME with the vision of transforming the lives of these young individuals. Through his innovative mentoring program, he has empowered thousands of indigenous students, breaking down barriers and providing them with the tools and support.

Bancroft's journey as a resilient leader has been marked by numerous challenges and obstacles. From navigating complex bureaucratic systems to overcoming skepticism he has consistently demonstrated resilience and determination. Bancroft's ability to adapt to adversity, remain focused on his mission, and rally support from unlikely connections and organizations has been instrumental in the success of AIME and his other endeavors.

Bancroft has transformed the traditional approach to mentoring and it's demonstrated throughout the organization as a core value to be "mentors, not saviors". Through AIME, he has created a platform for cross-cultural and generational collaboration, fostering understanding, and empathy, at the intersections of universal imagination, mentoring, and custodianship. His work has not only impacted the lives of Indigenous youth but has also influenced systems designers worldwide, inspiring new approaches to better relations with one another with an emphasis on our relationship with nature.

In addition to his practical work as Founder of AIME, Bancroft is an accomplished author and journalist. In *Hoodie Economics*, he explores over 60,000 years of Australian Indigenous wisdom to be at the forefront of approaches to challenge traditional economic models. His insights and ideas have sparked important conversations around the intersection of business, education, and social change. Bancroft's advocacy for Indigenous rights and educational equality has amplified the voices of marginalized communities and inspired others to take action through imagination and systems designs.

From where I stand, one of the most remarkable aspects of Jack Manning Bancroft's leadership is his ability to inspire and empower others to connect with those who are unlikely and to think about patterns that drive our daily decision-making. His infectious enthusiasm, relentless pursuit of social justice, and genuine care for the planet have motivated individuals like myself and organizations to join a digital nation called IMAGI-Nation. Bancroft's leadership style emphasizes collaboration, empathy, and inclusivity, supporting a network of change-makers who are dedicated to creating a more relational world.

Jack Manning Bancroft's journey as a resilient leader is still being defined by his visionary thinking, unwavering commitment to social change, and ability to inspire others to action. Through his work with AIME, he has challenged conventional approaches to how we interact with one another and with nature.

Chapter 13

DEAR RESILIENT LEADER: EMBRACE YOUR JOURNEY

Dear Resilient Leaders,

I hope that this email finds you confident and emboldened in your role as unwavering leaders. Today, I want to take a moment to reflect on the significance of your journey and the profound impact you have on those around you.

Leadership is a transformative undertaking. You will find yourself constantly evolving, and the path itself constantly changing. It demands courage, adaptability, and an unwavering commitment to personal growth. As resilient leaders, you exemplify these qualities and inspire others to persevere in the face of adversity.

Remember to take time to pause, reflect, and evaluate your leadership practices. Celebrate your achievements, while also embracing areas that require development. By acknowledging both your strengths and opportunities for growth, you can enhance your leadership effectiveness and inspire those you lead.

Your journey as a resilient leader is deeply intertwined with the growth and well-being of your team. Acknowledge the importance of fostering an inclusive and supportive work environment, where individuals are empowered to reach their full potential. Encourage open communication, provide mentorship, and create opportunities for professional development. By investing in your team's success, you cultivate a culture of resilience and collective achievement.

As you navigate your leadership journey, maintain a growth mindset. Embrace challenges as opportunities for learning and innovation. Encourage experimentation, promote calculated risk-taking, and view failures as valuable lessons on the path to success. Your resilience in the face of setbacks inspires your team to persevere and fuels a spirit of continuous improvement.

Furthermore, remember to nurture your own well-being along this journey. Prioritize self-care, maintain a healthy work-life balance, and seek support when needed. By taking care of your physical, mental, and emotional health, you set a powerful example for your team and ensure that you can lead with clarity, compassion, and energy.

As I close this email, Dear Resilient Leaders, I encourage you to wholeheartedly embrace your leadership journey. Reflect on your experiences, celebrate your growth, and remain dedicated to your own development as well as the success of those you lead. Through your resilience, you possess the power to create positive change, inspire others, and shape a future characterized by collaboration, innovation, and growth.

Wishing you continued success and fulfillment on your remarkable journey as resilient leaders.

Best regards,

Jacqueline V. Twillie
Founder of ZeroGap.co
Creator of the Resilient Leaders Program

EMBRACING RESILIENT LEADERSHIP: RESILIENT ORGANIZATIONAL CULTURE

Resilient leadership, accompanied by a resilient organizational culture, is crucial for navigating uncertainties and achieving long-term goals. This section explores the importance of embracing resilient leadership and cultivating a resilient organizational culture to foster growth, innovation, and sustained excellence.

The essence of resilient leadership is characterized by leaders who possess a strong sense of purpose, adaptability, and the ability to inspire and guide their teams through adversity, we've established that throughout the book. These leaders embrace change as an opportunity for growth, possess a growth mindset, and foster an environment of continuous learning. They demonstrate emotional intelligence, empathy, and the ability to communicate effectively, which helps build trust and promote collaboration within the organization.

Resilient leadership alone is not enough; it must be accompanied by a resilient organizational culture. Here are key elements to cultivate a culture of resilience within an organization:

A clear vision and purpose provide team members with a sense of direction and meaning. It helps align their efforts and instills a sense of focus in the face of challenges. Leaders should communicate the organization's purpose effectively and ensure that it is understood. Transparent and open communication is crucial for building trust and fostering resilience. Resilient Leaders should encourage honest and constructive dialogue, creating an environment where employees feel comfortable sharing their ideas, concerns, and feedback. This open communication helps identify potential issues early and enables prompt action. A resilient organizational culture embraces a growth mindset inclusive of continuous learning and adaptation. Leaders can encourage experimentation, innovation, and a willingness to take calculated risks. By encouraging employees to learn from failures and view setbacks as opportunities for growth, leaders create an environment that promotes resilience and creative problem-solving without fear of trying something new.

Resilient leaders empower their teams by delegating authority, providing autonomy, and encouraging collaboration. By involving employees in decision-making processes and valuing diverse perspectives, leaders foster a sense of ownership and collective responsibility. This collaborative approach enhances problem-solving abilities and helps the organization adapt swiftly to changing circumstances.

Resilience is closely linked to employee well-being. Leaders should promote work-life balance, provide resources for stress management, and establish support systems to help employees navigate personal and professional challenges. A workforce that feels supported and valued is more likely to exhibit resilience in the face of adversity.

A resilient organizational culture has numerous benefits to the health of an organization, including a resilient culture that enables organizations to adapt swiftly to changing market conditions, technological advancements, and unforeseen disruptions. It fosters the ability to seize opportunities and mitigate risks effectively. Resilient cultures encourage creativity, experimentation, and the freedom to take calculated risks. Employees feel empowered to think outside the box, leading to innovation and the development of new solutions and approaches.

When employees feel valued, empowered, and supported, their engagement and productivity levels increase. A resilient culture promotes a sense of purpose, fosters strong relationships, and boosts employee morale, leading to higher levels of commitment and performance.

Organizations with a resilient culture become attractive places for top talent. Employees seek environments that encourage growth, provide opportunities for personal and professional development, and foster a supportive atmosphere. Resilient organizations are more likely to retain their best employees and attract new ones.

Embracing resilient leadership and cultivating a resilient organizational culture is vital for organizations to thrive in today's dynamic business environment. By fostering a culture that values adaptability, continuous learning, collaboration, and employee well-being, leaders can build a resilient organization capable of embracing challenges, driving innovation, and achieving sustainable success in the long run. Resilient leaders and cultures set the stage for a resilient and prosperous future.

TAKING ACTION: APPLYING RESILIENT LEADERSHIP PRINCIPLES IN YOUR JOURNEY

Congratulations on completing this book and gaining insights into the principles of resilient leadership! Now, it's time to put your knowledge into action and apply these principles in your own leadership journey. This action plan serves as a roadmap to help you integrate resilient leadership into your daily practices and create a lasting impact.

Take time to reflect on your current leadership style and identify areas where you can incorporate resilient leadership principles. Consider your strengths and areas for development. Reflect on how you can leverage your strengths to inspire resilience in yourself and others, while also addressing any areas that need improvement.

Clarify your purpose as a leader and the vision you have for your team or organization. Articulate your purpose and vision in a way that inspires and aligns your team members. Communicate it consistently, allowing everyone to understand their role in achieving the collective goals and fostering resilience.

Create an environment of open communication where team members feel comfortable expressing their thoughts, concerns, and ideas. Encourage active listening and constructive feedback. Practice empathy and respond to challenges and feedback with a solutions-oriented mindset. Embrace diverse perspectives to foster innovation and resilience.

Promote a culture of continuous learning and growth. Encourage your team members to embrace challenges as opportunities for learning and development. Foster a safe space for experimentation, where calculated risks are encouraged and failures are viewed as valuable learning experiences. Provide resources and support for ongoing professional development.

Empower your team members by delegating authority and providing them with autonomy. Trust in their abilities and encourage them to take ownership of their work. Foster a sense of responsibility and accountability, while providing guidance and support when needed. Empowered team members are more resilient and motivated to achieve their goals.

Recognize the importance of employee well-being and prioritize it within your team or organization. Encourage work-life balance, promote stress management techniques, and provide resources for mental and emotional support. Lead by example by practicing self-care and prioritizing your own well-being. A healthy and resilient team is a productive one.

Model resilient behavior and lead by example. Demonstrate adaptability, perseverance, and a positive attitude in the face of challenges. Inspire your team members to embrace change, view setbacks as opportunities, and learn from failures. Celebrate successes and recognize the efforts and resilience demonstrated by your team.

Regularly assess your progress as a resilient leader and evaluate the impact of your actions on your team and organization. Seek feedback from team members and stakeholders to identify areas of improvement. Be open to adjusting your approach and strategies as needed, staying adaptable and responsive to changing circumstances.

Create an organizational culture that values resilience, collaboration, and growth. Reinforce resilient leadership principles through consistent communication, recognition, and rewards. Encourage teamwork, knowledge sharing, and cross-functional collaboration. Continuously nurture and strengthen the resilience of your organization as a whole.

Celebrate milestones and successes along the way. Recognize and appreciate the efforts of your team members in embodying resilient leadership principles. Celebrate their resilience, innovation, and growth. By acknowledging and celebrating achievements, you reinforce the importance of resilient leadership and inspire continued excellence.

Remember, applying resilient leadership principles is an ongoing process that requires commitment and continuous effort. Use this action plan as a guide, adapt it to your specific context, and keep pushing yourself and your team to reach new heights of resilience and success. Your journey as a resilient leader will shape not only your own growth but also the growth and resilience of those you lead. Best of luck in your resilient leadership journey!

The R4 Framework Checklist: Risk, Resilience, Reward, and Reset

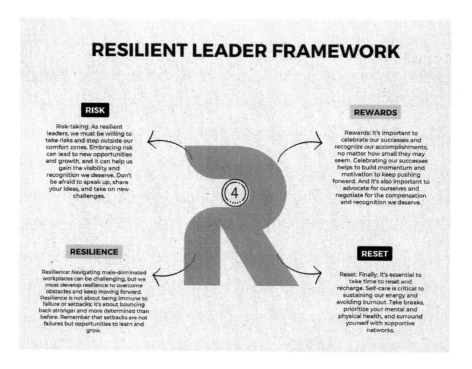

Risk Assessment:

- Identify and analyze the risks associated with the challenge or change you face.

- Consider the potential areas of stress or adverse outcomes that may arise.

- Evaluate the possibility, likelihood, and potential impact of each risk.

- Determine the level of exposure and decide if the risks are acceptable or if mitigation strategies are needed.

Resilience Building:

- Develop strategies to enhance resilience when facing challenges or changes before you need them.

- Cultivate a mindset of resilience by focusing on strengths, adaptability, and problem-solving skills.

- Build a support network of individuals or resources to assist and guide during difficult times.

- Foster a positive and resilient organizational culture that encourages learning from setbacks and encourages innovation.

Seeking Rewards:

- Clearly define the rewards or desired outcomes you aim to achieve.

- Set measurable goals and objectives that align with the challenges or changes you are navigating.

- Identify the actions, strategies, or initiatives that can lead to realizing those rewards.

- Implement a plan to track progress, measure success, and celebrate achievements.

Reset:

- Recognize the importance of rest and self-care in maintaining overall well-being and sustaining long-term success.

- Allow time for reflection and introspection to learn from experiences and adjust for future challenges.

- Encourage a culture that supports work-life balance and prioritizes mental and physical well-being.

- Take breaks, engage in activities that recharge your energy, and practice mindfulness or other relaxation techniques.

SHAPING THE FUTURE: INSPIRING, EMPOWERING, AND UPLIFTING OTHERS

Resilient leaders, especially those who have experienced being underrepresented, have a unique opportunity to shape the future by inspiring, empowering, and uplifting others. As you reflect on what you've learned from this book, I encourage you to ask yourself how you can contribute to creating a world where underrepresented leadership is no longer a problem to be solved. Consider the following questions:

How can I use my experiences as an underrepresented leader to inspire others?

Reflect on your journey and the obstacles you have overcome. How can you share your story and experiences to inspire and motivate others facing similar challenges? Consider mentoring, speaking engagements, or creating platforms to amplify diverse voices and perspectives.

How can I empower and support fellow underrepresented leaders?

Think about the specific challenges that underrepresented leaders face and consider how you can provide support. Are there networks or communities you can create or join to offer mentorship, guidance, or resources? Can you advocate for diversity and inclusion initiatives within your organization or industry?

How can I uplift and amplify underrepresented voices?

Recognize the importance of representation and inclusivity. How can you actively seek out and uplift underrepresented voices within your organization or community? Are there opportunities to promote diverse talent, collaborate with diverse teams, or create platforms for underrepresented individuals to share their expertise and perspectives?

How can I contribute to changing systems and structures that perpetuate underrepresentation?

Consider the systemic barriers that contribute to underrepresentation. How can you use your influence and position to advocate for change? Are there opportunities to participate in diversity and inclusion initiatives, policy discussions, or community engagement efforts that address systemic inequalities?

How can I foster a culture of inclusivity and belonging within my sphere of influence?

Reflect on the culture within your organization or community. How can you actively promote inclusivity, diversity, and belonging? Are there practices or policies that can be revised or implemented to create a more equitable environment? Can you engage in conversations and initiatives that challenge biases and promote fairness?

Remember, creating lasting change requires collective effort. Collaborate with others who share your vision of a world where underrepresented leadership is no longer a problem to be solved. Together, you can make a meaningful impact and shape a future that celebrates and values diverse leadership.

YOUR RESILIENT LEADER PROFILE

Dear Resilient Leader,

I cordially invite you to embark on a transformative journey of self-discovery and reflection by creating your very own Resilient Leader profile. In a world that demands strength, adaptability, and unwavering determination, it is crucial to understand the qualities that make you an exceptional leader.

To assist you in this empowering endeavor, I have compiled a series of fill-in-the-blank questions designed to uncover the depths of your resilience, guiding you toward a profound understanding of your unique leadership style. I encourage you to reflect deeply on each question and respond with utmost honesty and introspection.

One of my most challenging professional experiences was _____.

When faced with setbacks or failures, I tend to _____.

The key values that drive my leadership philosophy are _____.

In times of uncertainty, I rely on _____ to make tough decisions.

My greatest source of motivation and inspiration comes from _____.

The strategies I employ to maintain a healthy work-life balance include _____.

When faced with conflict or disagreement, my approach is to _____.

A memorable moment that showcased my resilience as a leader was _____.

The most significant lesson I have learned from a past mistake is _____.

My preferred method of nurturing and developing the resilience of my team members is _____.

The one thing I believe sets me apart as a resilient leader is _____.

If I could offer one piece of advice to aspiring resilient leaders, it would be _____.

I eagerly anticipate your thoughtful responses to these fill-in-the-blank questions, which will undoubtedly provide valuable insights into the remarkable leader you are. As you embark on this journey of self-discovery, may you uncover hidden strengths, recognize areas for growth, and inspire others through your unwavering resilience.

Please feel free to share your completed Resilient Leader profile with me or engage in further discussions on leadership and resilience. I believe in your ability to lead with resilience and make a profound impact on those around you.

With anticipation and admiration,

Jacqueline V. Twillie
Founder of ZeroGap.co
Creator of the Resilient Leaders Program

Made in the USA
Middletown, DE
21 March 2024